ISRAEL AT 75
Commemorative Edition

Hebrew Words

You Need to Understand The Bible

By Rabbi Akiva Gersh
Edited by Rabbi Elie Mischel

This book contains the name of God and should be treated with the same respect as a Bible.

75 Hebrew Words You Need to Understand The Bible First Edition, 2023

The Israel Bible was produced by Israel365 in cooperation with

Teach for Israel and is used with permission from

Teach for Israel. All rights reserved.

The English translation was adapted by Israel365 from the JPS Tanakh Copyright O 1985 by the Jewish Publication Society. All rights reserved.

Cover design and typesetting: Chani Gordon

Photo credits: Contains some images from frocksinstock.com

All rights reserved. No part of this publication may be reproduced, stored in a retrieval system or transmitted in any form or by any means, electronic, mechanical, photocopying, or otherwise, without the prior permission of the publisher, except in the case of brief quotations embedded in critical articles or reviews.

ISBN 978-1-957109-47-3, softcover

75 Hebrew Words You Need to Understand The Bible is a holy book that contains the name of God and should be treated with respect.

Preface

Rabbi Tuly Weisz

When the Babylonians destroyed the First Temple in Jerusalem in 586 BCE, the Jewish people were expelled from Judea for the first time. Though other peoples exiled from their homelands quickly assimilated into other societies and disappeared, the Jewish experience would prove to be anything but normal.

After 70 years of exile, most Jews settled into life in the Persian empire. Many Jewish men married Persian women, and many Jewish women married Persian men. When Cyrus the Great granted permission to the Judean refugees to return to Jerusalem and rebuild their destroyed Temple, only a small percentage chose to go home.

The few who did return to Israel were the poorest and least educated Jews, who had not acclimated well in Persia. The Bible tells us that those who followed Ezra and Nehemiah back to Israel were hardly an inspiring group of pioneers. Even those who chose to return to Israel were ignorant of their heritage and didn't even know the language of Judea. In just seventy years, they had forgotten how to speak Hebrew:

"A good number of their children spoke the language of Ashdod and the language of those various peoples, and did not know how to speak Judean." (Nehemiah 13:24)

Miraculously, this poor and ignorant group of pioneers would ultimately reclaim their Jewish identity, rebuild the Temple and learn to once again speak the language of their forefathers.

For those who appreciate the Bible as a living text that teaches much more than our ancient history, this observation is striking. The Book of Nehemiah perfectly describes the modern return of the Jews to Israel in the late 19th and early 20th centuries!

The pioneers who first returned to Palestine just over a century ago were mainly secular Jews. At the time, Russian Jews spoke Russian, German Jews spoke German, and French Jews spoke French. Like their ancestors, over the course of centuries of exile they too had forgotten how to speak Hebrew, a language that was relegated to prayer and study. Incredibly, one man changed all of that, and accomplished something unprecedented in human history.

Eliezer Ben-Yehuda (1858-1922) was born in Belarus and immigrated to Palestine in 1881. He was a newspaper editor and Hebrew lexicographer and decided that "in order to have our own land and political life it is also necessary that we have a language to hold us together." Using the Bible as his guide, he began writing a modern Hebrew dictionary, inventing new words when necessary. He insisted that the new schools opening in Israel teach their students in Hebrew and that others begin to speak the language as well.

Many scoffed at Ben-Yehuda's epic vision, but thanks to his steadfast determination, Hebrew has been revived from the dustbin of history and is now the official language of the State of Israel. Millions of Israeli Jews converse in Hebrew, conduct their daily affairs in Hebrew, and can read the Bible in the original Hebrew, their mother tongue.

Never before in human history has an ancient language been revived and brought back to life!

The volume you hold in your hand, *75 Hebrew Words You Need to Understand the Bible,* was published by Israel365 in honor of Israel's 75th anniversary and is a testament to God's fulfillment of His eternal promises to Israel. Rabbi Elie Mischel and Rabbi Akiva Gersh have done an outstanding job of selecting Hebrew words and finding insightful and inspirational lessons for those of us who are eager to connect with and understand God's holy words.

The miraculous rebirth of Hebrew symbolizes the revitalization of the Jewish people in the Land of Israel. Let us never take this miracle for granted!

Rabbi Tuly Weisz
Beit Shemesh, April 2023 / Nissan 5783

God's Holy Tongue: An Introduction to the Hebrew Language

Rabbi Elie Mischel

Though it has not yet received the attention it deserves, we are living through the beginnings of an extraordinary change among non-Jews who believe in the Bible. Across the world, individual seekers and thoughtful groups of believers have independently reached the same conclusion. Many thousands now understand that to understand the deeper meaning of the Bible, they need the key that will unlock its treasures: *the Hebrew language.*

For almost two millennia, the vast majority of Bible believers have studied the Bible in translation. From the Greek Septuagint to the Tyndale and King James translations into English, these translations literally changed the world, opening up the Bible to millions of people who otherwise could not access God's word. Translations of the Bible enabled the conversion of much of the pagan world to monotheism.

But alongside the benefits of translation came significant downsides. Even the very best translations of the Bible cannot capture the untold number of insights and allusions that can be gleaned from the original Hebrew. Each Hebrew word carries multiple meanings and often shares a grammatical root with other Hebrew words, weaving a web of meaning that is lost in translation. Later prophets frequently allude to earlier Biblical events by adopting words and phrases from earlier books and applying them in a different context. In translation, all of this subtlety and complexity is lost.

Most significantly, the inability of 99% of the world's believers to read the Bible in its original language means that huge numbers of Christians do not realize that the Hebrew Bible is a *Jewish* book about the *Jewish* people, written in the *Jewish* language, about events that took place almost exclusively in the *Jewish* homeland. Inevitably, this leads to a skewed understanding of the Hebrew Bible, and a lack of appreciation for both Judaism and the Jewish people. In other words, had Christians throughout the centuries understood the Bible in its original Hebrew, the history of Jewish-Christian relations would likely be a much happier story.

The remedy, as Marvin Wilson writes, is to study the Bible as a Jewish book, appreciating its language and its people. "Many Christians study the Old Testament only through the eyes of the New Testament... Christians typically believed they had no ongoing need of Jews and Judaism... But if Christians *began* with the Old Testament before moving to the New, they would come to understand the rich historical, linguistic, and cultural background which [the Hebrew Bible] constitutes on its own" (Wilson, *Our Father Abraham: Jewish Roots of the Christian Faith*).

THE UNIQUE POWER OF HEBREW

According to the mystical Kabbalistic work *Sefer Yetzirah*, the "Book of Creation," God created the world by literally *speaking* it into existence with the Hebrew language. Each individual letter of the Hebrew alphabet is imbued with spiritual energy, allowing it to serve as a vessel for creation. In other words, the Kabbalists believe that the spiritual foundation of the entire universe is rooted in the Hebrew alphabet.

The Kabbalists explain that the Tabernacle and its holy vessels were also constructed in this way. "See, I have called by name Bezalel the son of Uri, the son of Hur, of the tribe of Judah, and I have filled him with the spirit of God, in wisdom, and in understanding, and in knowledge, and in all manner of workmanship" (Exodus 31:2-3). The Kabbalists believe that when God filled Bezalel with the spirit of God, He taught him how to combine Hebrew letters, thereby giving him the power to construct the Tabernacle.

Unlike other languages, the Hebrew language does not arbitrarily assign words to objects, but rather reflects the essence of each object it describes. Take, for instance, the name given to Man, "*Adam*," which is derived from the Hebrew word "*adama*" meaning the "earth" or "soil" from which he was created. This signifies that Man has the potential for growth, much like a seed planted in soil. In contrast, the Hebrew word for animal, "*beheima*," is a combination of "*bah*" (in it) and "*mah*" (what), implying that the essence of an animal is already inherent within it. While an animal may undergo physical growth, its spiritual potential has already been realized.

In recognition of the unique richness and meaning of Hebrew, we thank God in prayer for "exalting Hebrew above all the other languages." Though human language is capable of articulating profound thoughts and intricate ideas, the people of Israel were blessed with the language of the Bible - a language that encompasses God's own wisdom and is ideally equipped to convey notions of sanctity.

At the beginning of human history, Hebrew did not belong exclusively to one nation, but to the entire world. "And the whole earth was of one language and of one speech" (Genesis 11:1). All of humanity spoke Hebrew! But instead of using their common language to join together in the *service* of God, the generation of the Tower of Babel joined together to *rebel* against God. The punishment for the people's sin of rebellion and failure to acknowledge God as Creator was to be scattered across the earth into many peoples and different languages, so that they could no longer communicate as one.

The day will come, however, when the peoples of the world will once again speak a common language. In the words of the prophet Zephania: "For then I will make the peoples pure of speech, so that they all invoke God by name and serve Him with one accord" (3:9). The great Medieval commentator Ibn Ezra maintains that the "pure speech" referred to by the prophet is the language of Hebrew, and that in future times the whole world will begin to learn Hebrew, the language of creation. This book is the beginning of the fulfillment of Zephania's prophecy!

A MIRACLE OF OUR TIME: THE REVIVAL OF HEBREW

Following the destruction of the Second Holy Temple in 70 CE, the Jewish people were scattered throughout the world, resulting in Hebrew gradually falling out of use as a spoken language in everyday life. However, with the return of Jews to the Holy Land in the 19th century, Hebrew was revived as a spoken language and currently serves as the primary language for nearly half of the Jewish population worldwide.

This unprecedented revival of Hebrew as a modern language is unparalleled in history - but it is only *one* of the many modern miracles surrounding the return of the Jewish people to the land of Israel that we have witnessed in our own generation! Since the emergence of modern Zionism in the late 19th century, one prophecy after another has been fulfilled. A broken people, decimated by the Holocaust, rose like a phoenix from the ashes. The desolate and devastated land of Israel was brought back to life. Jews from over a hundred countries all over the world have returned home in the greatest ingathering in the history of mankind. After centuries of foreign control, the holy city of Jerusalem is now unified and serves as the capital of the Jewish state. All of this was foretold by God in the Bible, and all of this has been fulfilled, before our eyes!

The flourishing of the state of Israel over the past 75 years since its founding in 1948, is nothing short of miraculous. After two thousand years of suffering and wandering, God's people can now hold their heads high once again!

To celebrate this modern miracle, we are proud to publish *75 Hebrew Words You Need to Understand the Bible*. Our hope and prayer is that this book will help those who do not know Hebrew appreciate the Bible in its original language, and begin to bridge the 1900 year chasm between Jews and Christians. This work will also serve as an essential companion to *The Israel Bible*, the world's first Hebrew Bible centered around the Land of Israel, the People of Israel, and the dynamic relationship between them.

May we soon see the day when God brings all those who attach themselves to Him to Jerusalem, where they will "rejoice in My house of prayer, their burnt offerings and sacrifices will be welcome on My altar, for My House shall be called a house of prayer for all peoples" (Isaiah 56:7).

ז **Zayin** 'Z'	ו **Vav** 'V'	ה **Hay** 'H'	ד **Dalet** 'D'
מ **Mem** 'M'	ל **Lamed** 'L'	ךְ **Final Khaf** 'KH'	כ **Khaf** 'KH'
ף **Final Pey** 'F'	פ **Fay** 'F'	פ **Pay** 'P'	ע **Ayin** Silent[1]
ת **Sav** 'T'	תּ **Tav** 'T'	שׂ **Sin** 'S'	שׁ **Shin** 'SH'

Notes:

If there is a vowel underneath the letter, the sound of the vowel is pronounced. If there is no vowel underneath, the letter remains silent.

[2] In Hebrew there are 2 types of Sh'vas. A Sh'va na is considered a vowel and is pronounced. This is represented in our transliteration by the apostrophe (') and pronouced like the 'e' in father. The other sh'va, the sh'va nakh, indicates the end of a syllable. It does not have its own sound, and therefore no phonetic representation.

[3] A kamatz katan looks like a regular kamatz but is pronounced like a kholam.

[4] The Hebrew alphabet has a unique feature known as gematriya , in which every letter is assigned a numerical value.

Above each letter is its numeric value[4]

אֻ/אוּ **Shuruk/Kubutz** 'u' junior	אֶ **Segol** 'e' in Edward
אְ **Sh'va**[2] ' (apostrophe)	אֵ **Tzayray** 'ay' in **day**

ג	ב	בּ	א
Gimel 'G'	Vet 'V'	Bet 'B'	Aleph Silent[1]
כ	י	ט	ח
Kaf 'K'	Yud 'Y'	Tet 'Tet'	Chet 'KH'
ס	ן	נ	ם
Samekh 'S'	Final Nun 'N'	Nun 'N'	Final Mem 'M'
ר	ק	ץ	צ
Raysh 'R'	Kuf 'K'	Final Tzadi 'TZ'	Tzadi 'TZ'

Vowels: The Aleph is silent[1] so we will use it in the example for each sound			
אִ	אָ	אַ	אָ
Kheerik Khasayr 'i' in **i**gloo	Kamatz Katan[3] 'o' in h**o**st	Patakh 'a' in hurr**a**h	Kamatz 'a' in hurr**a**h
אִי	אֹ/אוֹ	אַי	אָי
Kheerik Malay 'ee' in str**ee**t	Kholam 'o' in h**o**st	Patakh + Yud 'ai' in **ai**sle	Kamatz + Yud 'ai' in **ai**sle

01

Animal בְּהֵמָה

Beheimah (b'-hay-MAH)

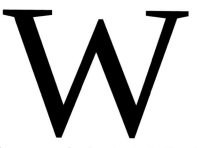

We first encounter the Hebrew word for animal, *beheimah*, in the opening chapter of Genesis, which describes the different kinds of animals created by God on the fifth day.

Beheimah refers specifically to domesticated animals like cows, sheep and goats, which were critically important to the early Israelites, many of whom were shepherds, including important leaders such as Abraham, Moses and King David. The Jewish Sages say that Moses was chosen by God to lead the Children of Israel because of how righteously and caringly he tended to his flock.

These domesticated animals would later become a key element of the Tabernacle and Temple service, where they were brought as daily sacrifices in the service of God. For an ancient Israelite, offering one of his animals as a sacrifice was like giving God a part of himself, creating a sense of closeness and connection to God.

The *beheimah* also appears prominently in the Bible's description of the kosher laws. Kosher animals cannot be predators and must have split hooves and chew their cud. Both of these conditions are met by cows, sheep and goats.

Although man is created in the image of God and has a higher level of soul than animals, the Bible requires us to treat animals with compassion, for they, too, are created by God. As Rabbi Moshe Cordovero (1522-1570) said: "One should respect all creatures, recognizing in them the greatness of the Creator. All creatures are imbued with the Creator's wisdom, which itself makes them greatly deserving of honor. If one were to disparage them, God forbid, this would reflect upon the honor of their Maker."

"God made wild beasts of every kind and **animals** of every kind, and all kinds of creeping things of the earth. And God saw that this was good."

(Genesis 1:25)

ויעש אלהים את חית הארץ למינה ואת
הבהמה למינה ואת כל רמש האדמה למינהו
וירא אלהים כי טוב.

"Of every pure **animal** you shall take seven pairs, males and their mates, and of every animal that is not pure, two, a male and its mate."

(Genesis 7:2)

מכל **הבהמה** הטהורה תקח לך שבעה שבעה
איש ואשתו ומן הבהמה אשר לא טהרה הוא
שנים איש ואשתו.

02

Ascent עֲלִיָּה

Aliyah (a-lee-YAH)

We first encounter *aliyah* when Joseph asks Pharaoh for permission to ascend to the land of Canaan to bury his father Jacob. "Please let me ascend and bury my father and return" (Genesis 50:5).

Joseph uses the word "ascend" not because the Land of Canaan (Israel) was at a higher physical elevation than Egypt, but because of its loftier spiritual status. For this reason, one who moves to the Land of Israel is said to be making *aliyah,* one who makes a spiritual elevation in his life.

Aliyah also describes the fulfillment of the commandment to ascend to Jerusalem to celebrate the three pilgrimage festivals of Passover, Shavuot and Sukkot. This is called aliyat ha'regel, "ascending for the festival," for traveling to the city of Jerusalem is considered a great spiritual elevation.

Another use of the word *aliyah* refers to one who is called up to make a blessing over the Torah scroll when it is read publicly. The platform from where the Torah scroll is read is usually a step higher than the synagogue floor, which helps the congregation hear the Torah reading better, reminding us that the Bible elevates us spiritually by bringing God's word into our lives.

The very last word in the Hebrew Bible is *ya'al,* a form of the word *aliyah* meaning "Let him ascend" (II Chronicles 36:23). Incredibly, the Hebrew Bible ends by highlighting the critical role that gentiles have played in helping the Jewish people ascend to and return home to Israel!

"My father made me swear, saying 'Behold, I am going to die. In my grave, which I dug for myself in the land of Canaan, there you shall bury me.' So now, please let me **ascend** and I will bury my father and then return."

(Genesis 50:5)

אבי השביעני לאמר הנה אנכי מת בקברי אשר כריתי לי בארץ כנען שמה תקברני ועתה **אעלה** נא ואקברה את אבי ואשובה.

"Thus said King Cyrus of Persia: Hashem, God of Heaven, has given me all the kingdoms of the earth, and has charged me with building Him a House in Jerusalem, which is in Judah. Any one of you of all His people, Hashem his God be with him and let him **ascend**."

(II Chronicles 36:23)

כה אמר כורש מלך פרס כל ממלכות הארץ נתן לי יהוה אלהי השמים והוא פקד עלי לבנות לו בית בירושלם אשר ביהודה מי בכם מכל עמו יהוה אלהיו עמו **ויעל**.

13

03

Awe

ירְאָה

Yirah (yir-AH)

Yirah, Hebrew for "awe," is most commonly used in the synonymous phrases *yirat Hashem* and *yirat shamayim*, meaning "awe of God." Awe is the foundation of serving God and connotes a powerful feeling of God's presence in one's life.

The word *yirah* is connected to the Hebrew word *lirot*, "to see." As we open our eyes and look at the world around us, we bear witness to God's majesty in nature as well as His involvement in all of the great events and mundane aspects of our world. When we open our eyes to truly see, we are inspired with awe, and ultimately love, for God.

Awe of God is essential to being a good person and also forms the basis of building a good society. That is why the Bible often adds the phrase "and you shall have awe of your God" after many commandments, for it is awe that leads one to follow God's righteous ways. This also explains why Abraham lied to Abimelech about Sarah being his sister, as he said, "surely there is no awe of God in this place, and they will kill me because of my wife" (Genesis 20:11).

The Sages teach that without awe, one cannot acquire wisdom. In the words of King David, "The beginning of wisdom is awe of God" (Psalms 111:10). Wisdom without awe of God is soulless knowledge. Only when one's understanding is rooted in awe of God does knowledge take on a higher purpose and lead a person to a more holy life.

"Abraham said: 'I thought, surely there is no **awe** of God in this place, and they will kill me because of my wife.'"

(Genesis 20:11)

ויאמר אברהם כי אמרתי רק אין **יראת** אלהים

במקום הזה והרגוני על דבר אשתי.

"The beginning of wisdom is **awe** of God; all who practice it gain sound understanding. Praise of Him is everlasting."

(Psalms 111:10)

ראשית חכמה **יראת** יהוה שכל טוב לכל

עשיהם תהלתו עמדת לעד.

04

Beauty

תִּפְאֶרֶת

Tiferet (tif-E-ret)

The Bible uses the word *tiferet*, Hebrew for "beauty" or "glory," to describe the special garments that the priests wore in the Tabernacle and the Temple during the performance of their service of God. These garments beautified the priests' appearance and brought glory to God through the presence of such beauty in His sanctuary.

"And He said to me, 'You are My servant, Israel in whom I glory'" (Isaiah 49:3). Though God is infinite and transcends this physical world, mankind can and must bring Him glory through holy deeds. When we beautify our service and worship of God, we bring God even greater glory.

The Sages teach, "Which is the straight path that a man should choose for himself? One which is *tiferet* to the person who follows it, and which also brings *tiferet* to him from others." This means our actions should be beautiful, both to us and to those observing us. By serving God with *tiferet*, we not only glorify God but also inspire others to do so as well.

In Kabbalistic thought, the attribute of *tiferet* is the "golden mean," representing the balance between the attributes of giving and kindness on the one hand, and the attributes of concealment and restraint on the other. There are times when we must give with abundant kindness, and there are times when love requires that we hold back and restrain ourselves from giving. Balancing these attributes requires great wisdom. This holy balance is represented by the attribute of *tiferet*, for it beautifies our world and glorifies God.

"Make sacral vestments for your brother Aaron, for dignity and **beauty**."

(Exodus 28:2)

ועשית בגדי קדש לאהרן אחיך לכבוד

ולתפארת.

"And He said to me, 'You are My servant, Israel in whom I **glory**.'"

(Isaiah 49:3)

ויאמר לי עבדי אתה ישראל אשר בך **אתפאר.**

05

Bible

Torah (to-RAH)

תּוֹרָה

Torah, Hebrew for "instruction," generally refers to the Hebrew Bible or, more specifically, the Five Books of Moses. Through its commandments and powerful stories of the lives of our forefathers and foremothers, the Torah is God's instruction book for how to live a life of holiness.

The numerical value of the word *Torah* is 611, just two shy of the number of commandments in the entire *Torah*, 613. The Sages explain the discrepancy by distinguishing between the first two of the Ten Commandments, which God spoke directly to the Israelites at Mount Sinai, and the other 611 commandments, which were heard exclusively by Moses, who then wrote them in the *Torah* and taught them to the nation.

According to Jewish tradition, there is both a Written *Torah* and an Oral *Torah*. The Written *Torah* comprises the text of the Five Books of Moses, while the Oral *Torah* is a collection of teachings that God gave to Moses that explain and elucidate the commandments and stories of the Written *Torah*. Without these oral teachings, the Written *Torah* would be incomplete and unclear. After the destruction of the Second Temple and the dispersion of the Jewish people throughout the world, the Oral *Torah* was put into writing because the Sages were concerned that its teachings would be forgotten and lost. Much of the Oral *Torah* was written in the books of the Mishnah and Talmud, the most important Jewish texts after the Hebrew Bible itself.

The Hebrew words for "teacher" and "parent" are *moreh* and *horeh*, two words that are linguistically related to the word *Torah*, for teachers and parents instruct their students and children in the ways of holiness, just as the *Torah* does for Israel and for all of humanity.

"God said to Moses, "Come up to Me on the mountain and wait there, and I will give you the stone tablets with the **Torah** and commandments which I have inscribed to instruct them."

(Exodus 24:12)

ויאמר יהוה אל משה עלה אלי ההרה והיה שם ואתנה לך את לחת האבן **והתורה** והמצוה אשר כתבתי להורתם.

"Moses charged us with the **Torah** as the heritage of the congregation of Jacob."

(Deuteronomy 33:4)

תורה צוה לנו משה מורשה קהלת יעקב.

06

Blessing

בְּרָכָה

Brachah (b'-ra-KHAH)

R eceiving *brachot*, blessings, is critically important in the Bible. Rebecca so desperately wanted Jacob to receive Isaac's blessing instead of Esau, she designed an entire plan to trick Isaac and ensure that Jacob received the blessing. At the end of his own life, Jacob blesses each of his sons. Moses, too, blesses each of the tribes of Israel before he dies.

Why are blessings so significant? A *brachah*, when given by a truly God-fearing person, is a powerful tool to manifest something in the world that is currently lacking. It opens up spiritual pathways for God's blessings to enter the world and change someone's life.

A second kind of *brachah* is found in the Bible as well: giving thanks to God for all we have and recognizing that God is the source of everything.

"And you shall eat, and you shall be satisfied, and you shall bless the Lord your God for the good land that He has given you" (Deuteronomy 8:10). This verse is the root of the Jewish practice to recite blessings before and after eating. One is forbidden to enjoy any of the pleasures of the world without first blessing God.

The grammatical root of the word *brachah* is *berech*, "knee," and connotes lowering ourselves to our knees in humility before God, emphasizing the importance of showing gratitude towards God.

Blessings are a means for directing us into the presence of God at all times, helping us maintain constant contact with our Creator. They are a remedy for forgetfulness, reminding us to continuously wonder at the grandeur of God's world.

"I will **bless** those who **bless** you and curse him that curses you; and all the families of the earth shall **bless** themselves by you."

(Genesis 12:3)

ואברכה מברכיך ומקללך אאר **ונברכו** בך כל משפחת האדמה.

"When you have eaten and are satisfied, you shall **bless** Hashem your God for the good land given to you."

(Deuteronomy 8:10)

ואכלת ושבעת **וברכת** את יהוה אלהיך על הארץ הטבה אשר נתן לך.

07

Bone

עֶצֶם

Etzem (*E-tzem*)

Upon encountering Eve for the first time, Adam declares that she is *etzem m'atzamai*, the "bone of my bones," for Eve was literally taken from the physical body of Adam. For this reason, *etzem* also means "essence," as Adam and Eve's unified state meant they shared a common essence. And so the Bible says in the very next verse, "Hence a man leaves his father and mother and clings to his wife, so that they become one flesh," returning to their original unified state in the Garden of Eden.

In one of the most vivid prophecies in the entire Bible, Ezekiel sees himself standing in a valley full of dry bones, where speaks to them and brings them back to life. These bones represent the "essence" of the Children of Israel, which is eternal and indestructible, and their coming back to life symbolizes their return to the land of Israel which, as we know, eventually takes place.

It's fitting, then, that *atzmaut*, the Hebrew word for "independence," also derives from *etzem*. Independence Day in the State of Israel is called *Yom Ha'Atzmaut*, marking the day when Israel returned to life as a free and independent nation.

Atzum, meaning "great" or "strong," also derives from *etzem*, for bones are the powerful and long lasting core of human strength. God uses this word to describe the great nation of Israel that will one day come from Abraham: "Abraham shall surely become a great and powerful (*atzum*) nation and all the nations of the earth are to bless themselves by him" (Genesis 18:18).

"This one at last is **bone** of my **bones** and flesh of my flesh. This one shall be called woman, for from a man was she taken."

(Genesis 2:23)

ויאמר האדם זאת הפעם **עצם מעצמי** ובשר
מבשרי לזאת יקרא אשה כי מאיש לקחה זאת.

"And He said to me, "Prophesy over these **bones** and say to them: O dry **bones**, hear the word of God!"

(Ezekiel 37:4)

תרמאו הלאה **תומצעה** לע אבנה ילא רמאיו
הוהי רבד ועמש תושביה **תומצעה** סהילא.

08

Bread

Lechem (LE-khem)

L echem, the Hebrew word for "bread," is often used to refer to food and sustenance more broadly, as in the verse from Psalms, "Who gives bread to all flesh, for His steadfast love is eternal (136:25).

In Judaism, bread represents the most complete and highest form of food, worthy of having a unique blessing recited over it: "Blessed are You, God, King of the universe, Who brings forth bread from the earth." Due to its elevated status, the Sages require us to ritually wash and purify our hands before eating bread, and on *Shabbat* and Jewish holidays, meals must include bread in order to reflect the elevated holiness of the day.

In the Tabernacle, and later in the Temple that stood in Jerusalem, special loaves of bread were baked each week and placed on golden tables opposite the *Menorah*, the golden candelabrum. These breads were called *lechem hapanim*, literally "bread of faces"; because the bread was baked in molds, the resulting loaves had two "faces," or sides. On the *Shavuot* holiday, a special offering of two loaves of bread were brought to celebrate and bless the harvesting of the new wheat crop.

Milchama, the Hebrew word for "war," contains the same letters as *lechem*, for it can often feel like a struggle, or "battle," to earn one's bread and make ends meet. For this reason, the miracle of the manna bread that God provided the Israelites for 40 years in the desert was also a test. The people were commanded to only collect the precise amount that they needed for each day and to trust that God would continue to provide *lechem* for them, day after day.

"And God said to Moses, "I will rain down **bread** for you from the sky, and the people shall go out and gather each day that day's portion—that I may thus test them, to see whether they will follow My instructions or not."

(Exodus 16:4)

ויאמר יהוה אל משה הנני ממטיר לכם **לחם** מן השמים ויצא העם ולקטו דבר יום ביומו למען אנסנו הילך בתורתי אם־לא.

"Who gives **bread** to all flesh, for His steadfast love is eternal."

(Psalms 136:25)

נתן **לחם** לכל בשר כי לעולם חסדו.

09

Charity

צְדָקָה

Tzedakah (tz'-da-KAH)

Tzedakah, Hebrew for "charity," is based on the grammatical root *tzedek*, meaning "justice." Superficially, "justice" and "charity" appear to be unrelated, but in Biblical thought they are intertwined. Giving charity is not merely a good deed; it is a Biblical obligation that we are obligated to fulfill whether or not we feel the desire to give. Justice obligates us to give a specified percentage of our income to the needy. In a just society, we must ensure that all people have the means to live a happy and productive life.

Similarly, a *tzaddik*, a "righteous person," is one who constantly strives to bring justice to the world. Many holy *tzaddikim*, righteous people, are particularly dedicated to giving *tzedakah*, distributing most, if not all, of their money to the poor.

The Bible highlights the importance of justice by repeating the word in the verse, "Justice, justice shall you pursue" (Deuteronomy 16:20). By specifically instructing us to *pursue* justice, the Bible teaches us that we must not be passive, for justice is neither natural nor easily accomplished. Justice will only be achieved through our continuous commitment and focused efforts.

One of God's seven Noahide laws for all of humanity requires the establishment of courts of justice. The Bible outlines specific laws regarding witnesses, testimony and the ways judges must preside over court cases, reflecting the critical importance of fair trials to a civilized society. While great efforts are made to achieve justice in all cases, human justice remains imperfect in comparison to the ultimate justice carried out by God, who sees all and "knows the secrets of the heart" (Psalms 44:22).

"**Justice, justice** shall you pursue, that you may thrive and occupy the land that your God is giving you."

(Deuteronomy 16:20)

צֶדֶק **צֶדֶק** תִּרְדֹּף לְמַעַן תִּחְיֶה וְיָרַשְׁתָּ אֶת הָאָרֶץ
אֲשֶׁר יְהוָה אֱלֹהֶיךָ נֹתֵן לָךְ.

"Zion shall be redeemed through judgment; her returnees, through **justice**."

(Isaiah 1:27)

הַקְּדַצְבַ הִיבְשׁוּ הַדְפַת טְפַשְׁמֵב וִיצַ.

10

Command מִצְוָה

Mitzvah (mitz-VAH)

28

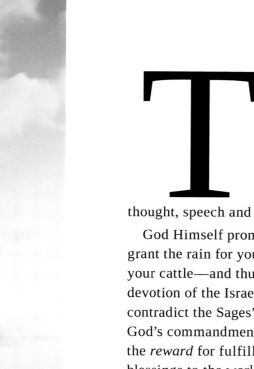

Though many are familiar with the word *mitzvah*, its meaning is generally misunderstood. *Mitzvah* does not mean "a good deed," as it is so often understood in popular culture, but rather "commandment." While all human beings must observe the seven *mitzvot* that God commanded to Noah, the people of Israel were given 613 commandments as part of their unique mission to bring Godliness into all aspects of our lives, through thought, speech and action.

God Himself promises that if the Israelites keep God's commandments, "I will grant the rain for your land in season" and "I will also provide grass in the fields for your cattle—and thus you shall eat your fill." (Deuteronomy 11:14-15). The spiritual devotion of the Israelites will bring physical blessing to the world. This appears to contradict the Sages' teaching that the Bible does not tell us the reward for keeping God's commandments. The Baal Shem Tov explains that the Bible is not telling us the *reward* for fulfilling God's commandments, but that nature will *naturally* bring blessings to the world when the Israelites follow God's word.

The *mitzvah* of wearing *tzitzit*, a four-cornered garment with fringes, reminds us of all of the commandments, as it says, "look at it and recall all the commandments of God and observe them" (Numbers 15:39). The numerical value of the Hebrew word *tzitzit* is 600. The fringes on each corner are doubled over to make 8 strings and those strings are tied into 5 sets of double knots. When we add 600, 8 and 5, we get 613, the total number of commandments in the Bible. By looking at the *tzitzit*, we recall all 613 of God's commandments.

"If, then, you obey the **commandments** that I **command** you this day, loving Hashem your God and serving Him with all your heart and soul."

(Deuteronomy 11:13)

והיה אם שמע תשמעו אל **מצותי** אשר אנכי **מצוה** אתכם היום לאהבה את יהוה אלהיכם ולעבדו בכל לבבכם ובכל נפשכם.

"That shall be your fringe; look at it and recall all the **commandments** of God and observe them, so that you do not follow your heart and eyes in your lustful urge."

(Numbers 15:39)

והיה לכם לציצת וראיתם אתו וזכרתם את כל **מצות** יהוה ועשיתם אתם ולא תתרו אחרי לבבכם ואחרי עיניכם אשר אתם זנים

11

Covenant

בְּרִית

Brit (b'-REET)

hen God chooses Abraham to be the father of a new nation that will bring His word to the world, He makes with him a *brit*, a "covenant." "On that day God made a covenant with Abram: 'To your offspring I assign this land'" (Genesis 15:18). This covenant was sealed by Abraham cutting a number of animals into two, which was an ancient way of making agreements between two parties. In fact, the Biblical word for cutting is *vater*, which is formed with the same letters as the word *brit*.

God's *brit* with the people of Israel is unchangeable. "And also the Glory of Israel will not lie nor repent; for He is not a man, that He should repent" (I Samuel 15:29). Even if the people of Israel stray or sin, God's covenant remains intact. A covenant with God is eternal; it is not a contract which loses its legitimacy if one or both of the sides breaks its conditions or promises.

Through His covenant with Abraham, God ensured that the land of Israel would belong to the people of Israel, for all time. Though the people of Israel sinned and were exiled from the land, their 1,900 years of wandering among the nations of the earth did not dissolve their bond with the land. For God promised that He would bring His people back: "He will bring you together again from all the peoples where *Hashem* your God has scattered you" (Deuteronomy 30:3).

The people of Israel's covenant with God is also expressed through the commandment to circumcise baby boys on the eighth day after birth. This is called a "*Brit Milah*," a "covenant of the foreskin," and it is a physical sign that attests to the baby's deep and unbreakable relationship with God.

"On that day God made a **covenant** with Abram:
"To your offspring I assign this land, from
the river of Egypt to the great river, the river
Euphrates."

(Genesis 15:18)

ביום ההוא כרת יהוה את אברם **ברית** לאמר
לזרעך נתתי את הארץ הזאת מנהר מצרים עד
הנהר הגדל נהר פרת.

"Such shall be the **covenant** between Me and you
and your offspring which you shall keep: every
male among you shall be circumcised."

(Genesis 17:10)

זאת **בריתי** אשר תשמרו ביני וביניכם ובין זרעך
אחריך המול לכם כל זכר.

12

Creation בְּרִיאָה

Beriah (b'-ree-AH)

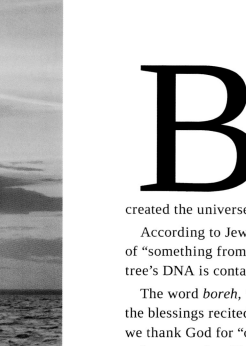**B**eriah, Hebrew for "creation," appears in its verb form (*barah*) as the second word in the Bible. "In the beginning God *created* heaven and earth."

Many Hebrew words are used to describe the making of something, but *beriah* is the only word that connotes creating something *ex nihilo,* from nothing. This form of creation occurred only one time in the history of the world, when God created the universe, creating something in a place where there was previously nothing.

According to Jewish thought, all things that came into being after this first creation of "something from nothing" were contained in this very first creation, much like a tree's DNA is contained in a tiny seed.

The word *boreh*, "Who creates," appears very often in Jewish blessings, specifically the blessings recited before eating food. When we eat vegetables, fruits, grains or wine we thank God for "creating" these foods so that we have the sustenance we need in order to survive. The word *boreh* is in the present tense, acknowledging that creation was not a one-time act of God, but rather the beginning of an ongoing process of providing for His world.

Bari, the Hebrew word for "healthy," contains the same Hebrew letters as the word *beriah*, creation. This teaches us that health and wellness is the intended and ideal state of all created things and that any experience of sickness is a temporary deviation from God's natural order.

"In the beginning God **created** heaven and earth."

(Genesis 1:1)

בראשית **ברא** אלהים את השמים ואת הארץ.

"I form light and **create** darkness, I make peace and **create** evil, I, Hashem, do all these things."

(Isaiah 45:7)

יוצר אור **ובורא** חשך עשה שלום **ובורא** רע אני
יהוה עשה כל אלה.

13

Death

מָוֶת

Mavet (MA-vet)

Though the Bible is focused almost exclusively on life and how to live in a righteous and Godly way, death is an inescapable reality and a necessary part of God's creation, as it says, "A time to give birth and a time to die" (Ecclesiastes 3:2).

There are many laws and rituals surrounding death, guiding us through our loved ones' final moments on this earth, burial, and how to properly mourn during the days, weeks and months after death. These laws include washing and purifying the body of the deceased, burying the dead as quickly as possible, sitting *shiva* for seven days at home to properly mourn the passing of a close relative, and reciting a special prayer called the *Kaddish* for eleven months after a relative's death to honor the deceased. These laws and rituals are critically important for mourners, guiding them and providing them comfort during the most difficult moments of life.

Though modern culture generally avoids serious discussion of death, an awareness of the inevitability of death and our limited time on this earth can help us live a more meaningful life. Life is short, and time is a precious commodity that we must appreciate and use to the fullest in our service of God.

At the end of days, during the era of redemption, God will resurrect the dead and fulfill Isaiah's prophecy: "He will swallow up death forever, and God will wipe away tears from off all faces, and the reproach of His people will He take away from off all the earth; for God has spoken it" (Isaiah 25:8). May we soon see that day.

"God spoke to Moses after the **death** of the two sons of Aaron who **died** when they drew too close to the presence of God."

(Leviticus 16:1)

וידבר יהוה אל משה אחרי **מות** שני בני אהרן בקרבתם לפני יהוה **וימתו.**

"I call heaven and earth to witness against you this day: I have put before you life and **death**, blessing and curse. Choose life—if you and your offspring would live."

(Deuteronomy 30:19)

העידתי בכם היום את השמים ואת הארץ החיים **והמות** נתתי לפניך הברכה והקללה ובחרת בחיים למען תחיה אתה וזרעך.

14

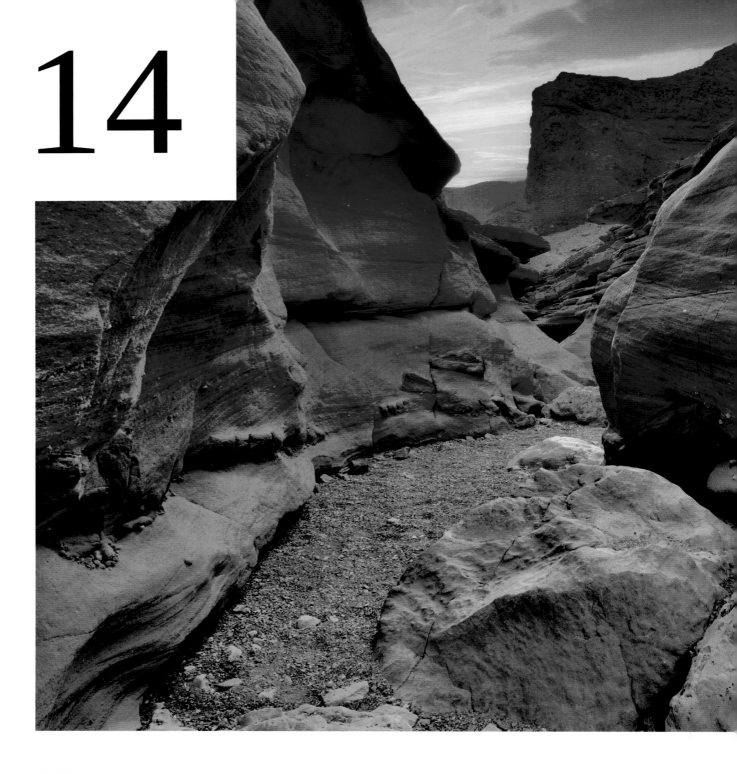

Desert

מִדְבָּר

Midbar (mid-BAR)

The desert, or *midbar* in Hebrew, plays a significant role in some of the most foundational stories in the Bible. All of the patriarchs were shepherds, spending much of their lives alone with their sheep in the desert. Moses' first encounter with God took place in the desert at the burning bush, and the children of Israel received the Torah in the desert at Mount Sinai. After fleeing from King Ahab, Elijah encountered God in a powerful spiritual experience at the very same mountain.

The grammatical root of *midbar* reflects its role as the setting for so many profound spiritual experiences. The same letters, in the very same order, can be pronounced as *midaber*, meaning "speaking." In the emptiness and quiet of the desert, the voice of God can be heard more clearly. When the noise of our everyday lives is removed, we can better hear the message that God is speaking to us.

Why did God give the Torah to the people of Israel in the desolate desert? The Sages explain: "Anyone who does not make himself ownerless, like the desert, cannot acquire the Torah." When we are full of ourselves, it is difficult to make space for the will and wisdom of God. Before we can receive the lofty spiritual wisdom of the Bible, we must humble and empty ourselves before God, like the desert.

Jewish tradition teaches that even before the Temple in Jerusalem was destroyed due to the nation's sins, God's presence left Jerusalem and settled in the desert. All who come to the desert seeking closeness to God with an open heart will find what they are looking for.

"Now Moses, tending the flock of his father-in-law Jethro, the priest of Midian, drove the flock into the **desert**, and came to Horeb, the mountain of God."

(Exodus 3:1)

ומשה היה רעה את צאן יתרו חתנו כהן מדין וינהג את הצאן אחר **המדבר** ויבא אל הר האלהים חרבה.

"On the third new moon after the Israelites had gone forth from the land of Egypt, on that very day, they entered the **desert** of Sinai. They journeyed from Rephidim and entered the **desert** of Sinai and encamped in the **desert**. Israel encamped there in front of the mountain."

(Exodus 19:1-2)

בחדש השלישי לצאת בני ישראל מארץ מצרים ביום הזה באו **מדבר** סיני. ויסעו מרפידים ויבאו **מדבר** סיני ויחנו **במדבר** ויחן שם ישראל נגד ההר.

15

Desire

Ratzon (ra-TZON)

רָצוֹן

I n Hebrew, *ratzon* means both "desire" and "will." As servants of God, we must do our best to make our actions desirable before God. We are also instructed to ensure our prayers are acceptable to God, as King David says, "May the words of my mouth and the prayer of my heart be desirable to You, God, my Rock and my Redeemer" (Psalms 19:15). This verse is recited at the end of many Jewish prayers as a request that our prayers be deemed fitting and acceptable before God.

The Sages teach, "Do His will as though it were your will," instructing us to align the way we live our desires with God's desires. In humility, we seek to nullify our own personal desires and fully accept God's will as our own.

The word *ratzon* is related to the word *yetzer*, meaning "inclination." Each of us possesses two internal inclinations that compete to guide and influence our everyday decisions and actions. There is the *yetzer ha'tov*, the positive inclination, and the *yetzer ha'ra*, the negative inclination. The quality of our lives is determined by how much we allow each of these inclinations to overpower the other.

The Hasidic teachers explain that "nothing stands before our desire." If we deeply and seriously desire to accomplish something in the realm of the spirit, nothing can prevent us from doing so! Our will is more powerful than we realize. When God sees that we truly desire holiness, He will help us achieve it.

"May the words of my mouth and the prayer of my heart be **desirable** to You, God, my rock and my redeemer."

(Psalms 19:15)

יהיו ל**רצון** אמרי פי והגיון לבי לפניך יהוה צורי וגאלי.

"I will bring them to My sacred mount and let them rejoice in My house of prayer. Their burnt offerings and sacrifices shall be **desirable** on My altar; for My House shall be called a house of prayer for all peoples."

(Isaiah 56:7)

והביאותים אל הר קדשי ושמחתים בבית תפלתי עולתיהם וזבחיהם ל**רצון** על מזבחי כי ביתי בית תפלה יקרא לכל העמים.

16

Egypt מִצְרַיִם

Mitzrayim (mitz-RA-yim)

The story of the nation of Israel is deeply connected to its experience in Egypt, known in Hebrew as *Mitzrayim*. The very first of the Ten Commandments mentions Egypt, as it says, "I am your God who brought you out of the land of Egypt, the house of bondage" (Exodus 20:2).

Why doesn't the first of the Ten Commandments say "I am your God who created the heavens and the earth"? Although God's role as Creator is central to our faith, the people of Israel did not witness the creation of the world, and so their knowledge of and belief in God is not rooted in creation. Rather, the nation of Israel was born through the miracles of the Exodus, when God overturned the laws of nature on behalf of His people. The Exodus is the firm foundation of our faith.

The word *Mitzrayim* is derived from the Hebrew word *tzar,* meaning "narrow" or "constricted." Ancient Egypt was a place of great spiritual constriction, for its people held strongly polytheistic beliefs and also believed that Pharaoh himself was a god.

In one of his most moving Psalms, King David uses a form of the word *tzar.* "From a place of constriction (*Min hameitzar*) I called on God. God answered me and brought me relief" (Psalms 118:5). The words of this verse are recited aloud on *Rosh Hashanah* just before the *shofar* is blown, for it beautifully represents both the shape of the *shofar,* narrow on one end, and the impact of its sound, awakening us from our personal slumber and spiritual constriction.

"You shall not oppress a stranger, for you know the feelings of the stranger, having yourselves been strangers in the land of **Egypt**."

(Exodus 23:9)

וגר לא תלחץ ואתם ידעתם את נפש הגר כי גרים הייתם בארץ **מצרים**.

"In **distress** I called on God. God answered me and brought me relief."

(Psalms 118:5)

מן **המצר** קראתי יה ענני במרחב יה.

Eternity

נֶצַח

Netzach (NE-tzakh)

Through two millennia of exile and degradation, *netzach*, the Hebrew word for "eternity," gave great strength and comfort to the people of Israel. The prophet Samuel refers to God as *Netzach Yisrael*, "The Eternal of Israel," when he tells King Saul that God's decision to take away his kingship for his failure to follow God's commands is final and will not be changed. More significantly, the combination of these two words, *Netzach* and *Yisrael*, reflects two essential truths: that God Himself is eternal, with no beginning and no end, and that God's covenant with and love for Israel is eternal, lasting and forever. Though God may punish the nation of Israel, He will never sever His relationship with His chosen people!

Netzach is also found at the beginning of many of the psalms in the form of *Lamnatzeach*, meaning "Conductor," as in the opening verse of Psalm 51: "For the Conductor, A psalm of David." As a conductor unifies a musical orchestra made up of different instruments, God unifies and brings order and purpose to the various contrasting and conflicting parts of His creation.

Netzach is also related to the word *nitzachon*, meaning "victory." The ultimate victory that we yearn for is the victory of good over evil. When that day comes, God's eternal greatness will be recognized by all of humanity, who will understand that God is the great Composer Who brings unity and purpose to all of creation.

"Yours, Hashem, are greatness, might, splendor, **eternity**, and majesty—yes, all that is in heaven and on earth; to You, Hashem, belong kingship and preeminence above all."

(I Chronicles 29:11)

לך יהוה הגדלה והגבורה והתפארת **והנצח**
וההוד כי כל בשמים ובארץ לך יהוה הממלכה
והמתנשא לכל לראש.

"Moreover, the **Eternal** of Israel does not deceive or change His mind, for He is not human that He should change His mind."

(I Samuel 15:29)

וגם **נצח** ישראל לא ישקר ולא ינחם כי לא אדם
הוא להנחם.

43

18

Extol

שֶׁבַח

Shevach (SHE-vakh)

Throughout the Book of Psalms, King David uses the Hebrew root *shevach*, "extol," or "praise," to express his love for God and his longing to draw closer to Him. Praising God is of such importance that every Jewish prayer service ends with a prayer of praise that begins with the words "It is upon us to praise the Master of all." Praising God helps us recognize His greatness and reminds us that He provides us with life.

This is why the Jewish morning prayer service begins with a selection of Psalms referred to as "Verses of Praise." Reciting the powerful words that King David used to praise God opens up our hearts and our souls to do the same, helping us begin each day with open eyes to see God's wonders in the world around us and God's providence in our lives. We are greatly indebted to King David for writing the Book of Psalms, which is most fundamentally a book of praise, so that we can always find the words we need to praise God.

"Praise God, all you nations, extol Him, all you peoples" (Psalms 117:1). King David describes a future reality in which the entire world, with its great diversity of peoples and nations, praises God. How will we achieve this ideal state? The Psalm continues: "For His love for us is great and the truth of the Lord endures forever. Hallelujah!" (Psalms 117:2). When humanity realizes how much God loves us and that God is the source of truth, conveyed to us through the Bible, all of mankind will be moved to praise Him.

"One generation shall **extol** Your works to another and declare Your mighty acts."

(Psalms 145:4)

דור לדור **ישבח** מעשיך וגבורתיך יגידו.

"Praise God, all you nations, **extol** Him, all you peoples."

(Psalms 117:1)

שבחוהו כל האמים.

19

Faith

אֱמוּנָה

Emunah (e-mu-NUH)

E*munah*, the Hebrew word for "faith" and "belief," is a foundational part of serving God and living a good life. We are meant to have faith in God and all of God's ways, accepting that there will always be things our minds cannot and will not understand. Faith begins where logic ends; our rational minds were not created with the capacity to understand everything.

One of the strongest aspects of faith is the belief in the coming of the Messiah and the Messianic Age. Maimonides, the great Medieval Jewish scholar, wrote a well-known formulation of this belief that is recited by Jews around the world: "I believe with perfect faith in the coming of the Messiah, and even though he may delay, I still wait for him everyday to come."

The prophet Habakkuk teaches that the end goal of the 613 commandments is faith. A righteous person does not live in order to have faith; it is his faith that gives him life! For faith is the source of all meaning and purpose in life.

Not only do we have faith in God, but God also has faith in us. Praising God, King David declared "Your faithfulness each night" (Psalms 92:3). The "night" David speaks of represents our moments of spiritual lowliness. Though we may doubt ourselves or even give up during these challenging times, God never gives up on us. As we declare in our very first words of prayer each morning: "I thank you, living and enduring King, for You have graciously returned my soul within me. '*Rabbah emunatechah*,' abundant is your faithfulness" - in us! We begin each new day by reminding ourselves how much God loves us and believes in our ability to succeed.

"To proclaim Your steadfast love at daybreak,
Your **faithfulness** each night."

(Psalms 92:3)

להגיד בבקר חסדך **ואמונתך** בלילות.

"Lo, his spirit within him is puffed up, not upright, but the righteous shall live by his **faith**."

(Habakkuk 2:4)

הנה עפלה לא ישרה נפשו בו וצדיק **באמונתו**
יחיה.

47

Festival

Regel (RE-gel)

רֶגֶל

Regel, Hebrew for "festival," refers to the three annual pilgrimage festivals: Passover, Shavuot and Sukkot. When the Temple stood in Jerusalem, Israelites were commanded to travel to Jerusalem during these festivals in order to stand in the presence of God in His holiest place. For many people, this journey could take a week or more. Pilgrims would then celebrate the festival for a full week in Jerusalem, before finally taking another week to return home. Though each pilgrimage required a significant investment of time and money, this experience was an essential part of ancient Jewish life. By celebrating the festivals together in the Temple, the people strengthened their bond with God and infused the rest of their year with Godliness and clarity of purpose.

The festivals coincide with different stages in the land of Israel's agricultural cycle. Passover is the Festival of Spring, when the crops have just begun to ripen. Shavuot is the Festival of the Harvest, occuring in the late spring during the harvest. Sukkot is the Festival of Gathering, and is celebrated in the fall when the crops are gathered. In Biblical life, spirituality and physicality go hand in hand.

Regel also means "feet" in Hebrew. Though seemingly unrelated to one another, the words "feet" and "festival" are bonded together through the people's pilgrimages to Jerusalem. Most pilgrims traveled to Jerusalem on foot, joyously undertaking the arduous journey to celebrate with God in Jerusalem. In this spirit, the Sages praise the pilgrims by citing a passage from Song of Songs: "How beautiful are your footsteps in your shoes, daughter of nobles" (7:2).

"Three times a year you shall hold a **festival** for Me. You shall observe the Feast of Matzah, eating matzah for seven days as I have commanded you at the set time in the month of Spring, for in it you went forth from Egypt; and none shall appear before Me empty-handed."

(Exodus 23:14-15)

שלש **רגלים** תחג לי בשנה. את חג המצות תשמר שבעת ימים תאכל מצות כאשר צויתך למועד חדש האביב כי בו יצאת ממצרים ולא יראו פני ריקם.

"And God said, "Do not come closer! Remove your sandals from your **feet**, for the place on which you stand is holy ground!"

ויאמר אל תקרב הלם של נעליך מעל **רגליך** כי המקום אשר אתה עומד עליו אדמת קדש הוא.

49

Funeral

Levaya (l'-va-YAH)

לְוָיָה

L evaya, Hebrew for "funeral," is derived from the verb "to escort." Jewish law obligates us to escort the body of the deceased all the way to the grave, to honor the person being buried.

We are also obligated to escort visitors upon their departure from our homes. Hosts are required to provide their guests with food, drink and "escort." Escorting guests out of one's home provides both physical and spiritual protection to people as they embark on their travels, a potentially dangerous endeavor in ancient times.

The Hebrew word l'halvot, "to lend," is derived from the same root as levaya. When we help others by lending them money at a time of need, we "escort" them through a difficult chapter in their lives.

The word *levaya* also shares the same root as Levi'im, the people of the tribe of Levi. The Levites had the special honor of working in the Temple in Jerusalem as gatekeepers, guards and musicians whose music accompanied, or "escorted," every sacrifice that was offered by the priests.

During the 40 years of the Israelites' journey through the desert, the people changed locations many times, requiring the Tabernacle to be dismantled and reconstructed with each move. The Levites were charged with carrying the various pieces and parts of the Tabernacle as the nation traveled, literally escorting the Tabernacle on its journey.

In the Land of Israel, the Levites were not allotted land like the other tribes, living instead in Levite cities scattered throughout Israel and subsisting on tithes and contributions. Their role was to serve as teachers to the rest of the nation and to escort them on their spiritual journeys through this world.

"You shall rejoice in your festival, with your son and daughter, your male and female slave, the **Levite**, the stranger, the fatherless, and the widow in your communities."

(Deuteronomy 16:14)

ושמחת בחגך אתה ובנך ובתך ועבדך ואמתך
והלוי והגר והיתום והאלמנה אשר בשעריך.

"He is always generous, and lends, and his children are held blessed."

(Psalms 37:26)

כל היום חונן **ומלוה** וזרעו לברכה.

22

God   אֱלוֹהִים

Elohim (e-lo-HEEM)

Elohim is one of the names of God that most commonly appear in the Bible. Simply understood, this name - the plural for "gods" - is deeply problematic. How can the world's first monotheistic faith refer to the Creator as "gods," in plural? But it actually makes perfect sense.

In ancient times, people treated the forces of nature as their gods, worshiping the sun, moon and stars, among other things. Abraham, who was raised in this pagan society, ultimately realized that all of these forces were actually under the control and will of one single God. He then began revealing this truth to all he encountered.

Abraham's descendants continued his work and mission. Famously, the prophet Elijah challenged 850 idolatrous priests of *Baal* on Mount Carmel. After a Godly fire came down and consumed Elijah's entire offering, the entire fell on their faces and cried out "*Elohim* is God, *Elohim* is God!" (I Kings 18:39). The people powerfully expressed their rediscovered belief that natural forces are *not* independent gods, but rather under the domain of the one true God.

This is illustrated beautifully by the numerical value of the word *Elohim*, 86, which is the same numerical value as the Hebrew word *ha'teva*, which means "nature." This connection reminds us that God both created and controls all that is in nature. There is nothing separate from him and all natural forces are tools He built into the creation of the world.

"When they saw this, all the people flung themselves on their faces and cried out: '**Elohim** is God, **Elohim** is God!'"

(Kings I 18:39)

וירא כל העם ויפלו על פניהם ויאמרו יהוה הוא האלהים יהוה הוא האלהים.

"And **Elohim** created mankind in the Divine image, creating it in the image of **Elohim**, creating them male and female."

(Genesis 1:27)

ויברא אלהים את האדם בצלמו בצלם אלהים ברא אתו זכר ונקבה ברא אתם.

53

23

Guard

שָׁמוֹר

Shamor (sha-MOR)

Shamor, Hebrew for "guard," is frequently used throughout the Bible to exhort the people of Israel to guard God's commandments. In the Ten Commandments, they are told to "guard" *Shabbat* as well as to "remember" Shabbat. To "guard" *Shabbat* means keeping the detailed laws of the holy day of rest, and so a Jew who observes the laws of *Shabbat* is known as a *shomer Shabbat*, "one who guards *Shabbat*." By contrast, "remembering *Shabbat*" means infusing *Shabbat* with holiness and spirituality.

The Sages explain that these two words, "guarding" and "remembering," were spoken by God simultaneously during the giving of the Ten Commandments, an impossible feat for human beings. For God, "guarding" and "remembering" *Shabbat* are equally important and combine to create the ideal experience of the day of rest.

Shamor also describes Adam's role in the Garden of Eden. "God settled man in the Garden of Eden, to work it and *guard* it" (Genesis 2:15). Adam was given permission to use the natural resources of the world for his own benefit. But alongside this gift, man was also given the responsibility to guard and protect God's world. As the Sages say, "When God created Adam, He said to him: 'See My creations, how beautiful they are. Make certain that you don't ruin and destroy My world, for if you destroy it, there will be no one to mend it after you.'"

Alone among all of God's creations, humanity has been entrusted with two holy tasks: to guard His word and to guard His world.

"**Guard** God's commandments and laws, which I enjoin upon you today, for your good."

(Deuteronomy 10:13)

לשמר את מצות יהוה ואת חקתיו אשר אנכי
מצוך היום לטוב לך.

"God settled the man in the Garden of Eden, to work it and **guard** it."

(Genesis 2:15)

ויקח יהוה אלהים את האדם וינחהו בגן עדן
לעבדה **ולשמרה.**

24

Hatred

Sinah (sin-AH)

Sinah, Hebrew for "hatred," stands in stark contrast to the Bible's commandments to love God and to love one's neighbor. According to the Sages, *Sinat hinam*, "baseless hatred," was the sin that led to the destruction of the Second Temple in Jerusalem by the Romans. They believed that the internal fighting among the Jews caused rifts within Judean society that physically and spiritually weakened the nation, ultimately leading to defeat and exile. The first Chief Rabbi of Israel, Rabbi Avraham Yitzhak HaKohen Kook, taught that since baseless hatred was the cause of the nation's destruction and exile, the only way to rebuild the nation and gather up th exiles of Israel is through *ahavat hinam*, "baseless" and unconditional love.

Sinah is linguistically related to the word *Sinai*, the mountain on which the nation of Israel received the Torah. When God gave His Bible to the people of Israel and selected them as His chosen nation, other nations became jealous of the Israelites and began to hate them. In the future, these nations will realize that by receiving God's Torah and keeping its commandments, the people of Israel bring God's blessings to the entire world.

"O you who love God, hate evil!" (Psalms 97:10). King David tells us not to hate the people who commit evil acts, but rather to hate the evil that they do. All human beings can repent for their wrongdoings, turn away from their evil ways and return to God with an open heart.

"She conceived again and bore a son, and declared, 'This is because God heard that I was **hated** and has given me this one also'; so she named him Simon."

(Genesis 29:33)

ותהר עוד ותלד בן ותאמר כי שמע יהוה כי **שנואה** אנכי ויתן לי גם את זה ותקרא שמו שמעון.

"O you who love God, **hate** evil! He guards the lives of His loyal ones, saving them from the hand of the wicked."

(Psalms 97:10)

אהבי יהוה **שנאו** רע שמר נפשות חסידיו מיד רשעים יצילם.

57

25

Heavens שָׁמַיִם

Shamayim (sha-MA-yim)

Shamayim, Hebrew for "heavens," appears in the very first verse of the Bible. "In the beginning God created the heavens and the earth." The Bible, however, tells us almost nothing about the creation of the heavens, focusing almost entirely on the creation of the Earth and on the lives of the people who inhabit it. "The heavens belong to God, but the earth He gave over to man" (Psalms 115:16). Our primary goal in life is not to understand the mysteries of the vast heavens, but rather to learn how to best live our daily lives here on Earth.

Nevertheless, the great medieval rabbi, Maimonides, favored the study of science and believed that contemplating God's wonders in nature brings people closer to love and awe of God. As is written in the Book of Psalms, "When I consider Your heavens, the work of Your fingers – what is man that You are mindful of him?" (Psalms 8:4-5).

The word *shamayim* contains within it the Hebrew word *mayim*, meaning "water." The atmosphere, or heavens, contains a significant amount of water, a fact reflected in the verse, "God made the expanse, and separated the water which was below the expanse from the water which was above the expanse" (Genesis 1:7).

Shamayim is also used to refer to God Himself. *Yirat shamayim*, "awe of God," literally means "fear of heaven." Similarly, performing an act for God's sake is called *l'shem shamayim*, "for the sake of heaven."

"Such is the story of **heaven** and earth when they were created, on the day God made earth and **heaven**."

(Genesis 2:4)

אלה תולדות **השמים** והארץ בהבראם ביום עשות יהוה אלהים ארץ **ושמים**.

"The **heavens** belong to God, but the earth He gave over to man."

(Psalms 115:16)

השמים שמים ליהוה והארץ נתן לבני אדם.

26

Hebrew

עִבְרִי

Ivri (iv-REE)

God's chosen people have gone by many names. They are referred to as "Israelites," the children of Jacob whose name was changed to Israel. And they are commonly referred to as Jews, for after the destruction of the first Temple and their exile to Babylonia, most of the Israelites who did not assimilate and disappear descended from the tribe of Judah. But before they received either of these names, they were known as *Ivrim*, "Hebrews."

What is the meaning of this name? Some explain that Abraham is referred to as an *Ivri* because he was a descendant of Eber. Others highlight the linguistic connection between *ivri* and the Hebrew word *Eiver*, meaning "side," for Abraham immigrated to Israel from the other "side" of the Jordan River, having come from the East.

A deeper message emerges from the connection between *Ivri* and *Eiver*. From a young age, Abraham was unlike any other people of his generation. As it related to religious beliefs, morality and ethics, it can be said that the whole world was on one side, and Abraham was on the other. He was not afraid to be different and didn't shy away from speaking out against evil. For him, living a life of truth mattered more than receiving the approval of others. This made Abraham worthy of bringing God's message to the world.

God tells Moses to refer to Him as the "God of the Hebrews" when he confronts Pharaoh and cries out, "Let my people go!" For by using this name, Moses conveyed a critical message to Pharaoh: that Moses' people were unlike any other nation! The Hebrews believed in God, and they would not be afraid to stand up against those who sought to oppress them, a strength they inherited from Abraham, the very first *Ivri*.

"A fugitive brought the news to Abram the **Hebrew**, who was dwelling at the terebinths of Mamre the Amorite, kinsman of Eshkol and Aner, these being Abram's allies."

Genesis 14:13)

ויבא הפליט ויגד לאברם **העברי** והוא שכן באלני ממרא האמרי אחי אשכל ואחי ענר והם בעלי ברית אברם.

"And say to him, the God of the **Hebrews** sent me to you to say, "Let My people go so that they may worship Me in the wilderness." But you have paid no heed until now."

(Exodus 7:16)

ואמרת אליו יהוה אלהי **העברים** שלחני אליך לאמר שלח את עמי ויעבדני במדבר והנה לא שמעת עד כה.

27

Heritage מוֹרָשָׁה

Morashah (mo-ra-SHAH)

Morashah, Hebrew for "heritage," is related to the Hebrew word *yerusha*, meaning "inheritance." In the Bible, God gave two great gifts to the nation of Israel as a heritage and an inheritance.

The first inheritance is the Bible itself. "Moses charged us with the Torah, as the heritage of the congregation of Jacob" (Deuteronomy 33:4). God gave the Torah to the nation of Israel as a special possession to be cherished, to guide them and help them fulfill their unique mission as God's chosen people. The Torah must be passed down from one generation to the next, and each generation must preserve it and safeguard it from being perverted by alien philosophies and worldviews. At the same time, the leaders of each generation must ensure that the masses of Israel preserve this holy heritage in their lives and do not assimilate and disappear into the broader population.

The second inheritance is the Land of Israel. "I will bring you into the land which I swore to give to Abraham, Isaac, and Jacob, and I will give it to you for a heritage, I am God" (Exodus 6:8).

Throughout the Bible, God tells the children of Israel that He will bring them to the Land of Israel as was first promised to Abraham, who faithfully left his birthplace in order to go there. Rashi, teaches that the Bible begins with God's creation of the world in order to emphasize that all existence belongs to God and that He can give the Land of Israel to whomever He chooses. God chose to give the land to the people of Israel as a heritage and inheritance, for it possesses unique spiritual qualities that will enable God's people to fulfill their unique mission.

"Moses charged us with the Torah, the **heritage** of the congregation of Jacob."

(Deuteronomy 33:4)

תורה צוה לנו משה **מורשה** קהלת יעקב.

"I will bring you into the land which I swore to give to Abraham, Isaac, and Jacob, and I will give it to you for a **heritage**, I am God."

(Exodus 6:8)

והבאתי אתכם אל הארץ אשר נשאתי את ידי לתת אתה לאברהם ליצחק וליעקב ונתתי אתה לכם **מורשה** אני יהוה.

28

Holiness   קְדֻשָּׁה

Kedushah (k'-du-SHAH)

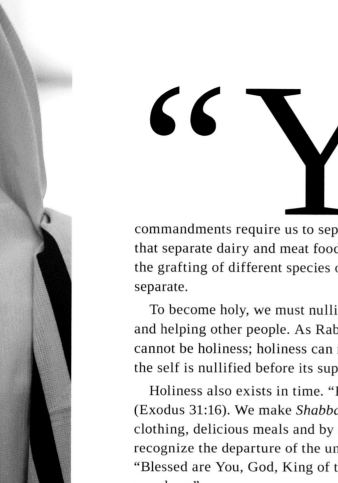

"**Y**ou shall be holy, for I, your God am holy" (Leviticus 19:2). The Hebrew word *kedushah* is generally used to describe "holiness." But Its root, *kadosh*, means "to be separate," for only when we distinguish between the holy and mundane can we experience holiness. Many of the Biblical commandments require us to separate one thing from another, such as commandments that separate dairy and meat foods, prohibit the weaving of wool and linen and forbid the grafting of different species of trees. A holy nation must learn to distinguish and separate.

To become holy, we must nullify our egos and dedicate ourselves to serving God and helping other people. As Rabbi Adin Steinsaltz wrote, "Where there is ego, there cannot be holiness; holiness can reside only where there is a surrender of the 'I,' where the self is nullified before its supernal source."

Holiness also exists in time. "Remember the day of *Shabbat* to make it holy" (Exodus 31:16). We make *Shabbat* different and holy through special prayers, fine clothing, delicious meals and by elevating our speech. At the end of *Shabbat*, we recognize the departure of the unique holiness of the day by reciting the blessing, "Blessed are You, God, King of the Universe, Who separates between the holy and the mundane."

The holiest place in the world is Jerusalem, the location chosen to build the Holy Temple for God, known as the *Beit HaMikdash*, the "House of Holiness." The name "House of Holiness" reflects the Bible's earlier command to build the Tabernacle, the predecessor to the Holy Temple. "And let them make Me a holy sanctuary that I may dwell among them" (Exodus 25:8).

"Speak to the whole Israelite community and say to them: You shall be **holy**, for I, your God, am **holy**."

(Leviticus 19:2)

דבר אל כל עדת בני ישראל ואמרת אלהם
קדשים תהיו כי קדוש אני יהוה אלהיכם.

"And let them make Me a **holy** sanctuary that I may dwell among them."

(Exodus 25:8)

ועשו לי מקדש ושכנתי בתוכם.

29

Honor

Kavod (ka-VOD)

כָּבוֹד

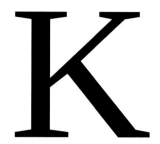

Kavod, Hebrew for "honor," appears in the fifth of the Ten Commandments when God directs us to honor our parents. Together with God, our parents gave us the greatest possible gift - our very lives! In Jewish law, children are obligated to actively honor their parents in many different ways, including feeding them and helping them get dressed when they grow old, not calling them by name and not sitting in their designated seat. Honoring one's parents is so important, it is one of only two commandments in the entire Bible rewarded with a promise of long life.

We are also instructed to give honor to others, even as we ourselves must flee from honor. The Talmud teaches: "Who is honored? The one who gives honor to others." By not focusing on our own honor and being concerned more with the honor of others, we become truly worthy of being honored! In particular, the Bible directs us to honor our elders: "You shall rise before the aged and show deference to the old" (Leviticus 19:32).

The Bible also instructs us to honor *Shabbat*. We do so by observing the many laws of *Shabbat*, wearing special clothes, and eating delicious foods. If one comes across a special food during the course of the week, it is proper to set it aside and eat it on *Shabbat*, to honor the holy day of rest. On *Shabbat* we recognize that God created the entire world and everything in it, and so by honoring *Shabbat*, we honor God.

"**Honor** your father and your mother, that you may long endure on the land that Hashem your God is giving to you."

(Exodus 20:12)

כבד את אביך ואת אמך למען יאריכון ימיך על האדמה אשר יהוה אלהיך נתן לך.

"He said, 'Oh, let me behold Your **honor**!'"

(Exodus 33:18)

ויאמר הראני נא את **כבדך**.

30

Horn

Shofar (sho-FAR)

שׁוֹפָר

Shofar, Hebrew for "horn," refers to the ram's-horn trumpet used throughout Jewish history in religious ceremonies and as a battle signal. Today, the *shofar* is primarily blown on Rosh Hashanah, the holiday celebrating the Jewish new year. The Bible refers to Rosh Hashanah as "the day of the *shofar* blast," since the blowing of the *shofar* is the central component and focus of the day. The blowing of the *shofar* recalls the ram that Abraham sacrificed in place of Isaac, reminding God of the merits of our holy forefathers.

Shofar is grammatically related to the Hebrew word *shipur*, meaning "improvement," for the sound of the *shofar* can awaken people and inspire them to improve their ways and realign their lives with the word of God. The prophet Amos asked, "When a ram's horn is sounded in a town do the people not tremble?" (Amos 3:6). When God gave the Bible to the children of Israel at Mount Sinai, the *shofar* blast shook them to their core: "On the third day, as morning dawned, there was thunder, and lightning, and a dense cloud upon the mountain, and a very loud blast of the *shofar*; and all the people who were in the camp trembled" (Exodus 19:16).

The *shofar* was used in ancient Israel on the day of Yom Kippur during the Jubilee year to proclaim freedom to all slaves and announce the returning of all lands to their original ancestral owners, for the *shofar* blast signals a new era has arrived. As the prophet Isaiah explains, the *shofar* will herald the ingathering of the exiles to Jerusalem and the final redemption. "And on that day, a great *shofar* shall be sounded… and they will come and worship God on the holy mount, in Jerusalem" (Isaiah 27:13).

"On the third day, as morning dawned, there was thunder, and lightning, and a dense cloud upon the mountain, and a very loud blast of the **shofar**; and all the people who were in the camp trembled."

(Exodus 19:16)

ויהי ביום השלישי בהית הבקר ויהי קלת וברקים וענן כבד על ההר וקל **שפר** חזק מאד ויחרד כל העם אשר במחנה.

"Then you shall sound the **shofar** loud; in the seventh month, on the tenth day of the month—the Day of Atonement—you shall have the **shofar** sounded throughout your land."

(Leviticus 25:9)

רושעב יעבשה שדחב העורת **רפוש** תרבעהו לכב **רפוש** וריבעת םירפכה םויב שדחל סכצרא.

69

31

House

בַּיִת

Bayit (BA-yit)

A bayit, a house, is a place that is familiar to us, where we feel comfortable and connected. We feel safe at home.

The word *bayit*, however, is used in Hebrew to describe more than just our personal dwelling spaces. It also refers to the most important buildings in all of Biblical history and ritual: the Temple that once stood in Jerusalem and our present-day synagogues.

The Temple was called the Beit HaMikdash, literally "the House of the Holy." Though it was elevated above all other physical structures and was located in the holiest place in the world, it was still meant to be and feel like an intimate home for all people. As Isaiah said, "My house shall be called a house of prayer for all nations" (Isaiah 56:7).

This idea is reflected in God's commandment to build the Tabernacle, the predecessor to the Temple. "Make for Me a Sanctuary and I will dwell among them" (Exodus 25:8). The verse says "dwell among them" instead of "dwell in it," emphasizing that the purpose of the Tabernacle was to create a place where humanity would feel at home with God.

The same is true of the Beit Knesset, the Hebrew word for synagogue, which literally means "a house of gathering." The synagogue is meant to simultaneously create an atmosphere of great awe and great closeness to God. As Rebbe Nachman of Breslov taught, "one should talk to God as if talking to a close friend." By experiencing the synagogue as a "house," we feel comforted and close to God, allowing us to open our hearts wide in prayer and in praise.

"I will bring them to My sacred mount and let them rejoice in My **house** of prayer. Their burnt offerings and sacrifices shall be welcome on My altar; for My **house** shall be called a **house** of prayer for all peoples."

(Isaiah 56:7)

והביאותים אל הר קדשי ושמחתים **בבית**
תפלתי עולתיהם וזבחיהם לרצון על מזבחי כי
ביתי בית תפלה יקרא לכל העמים.

"Shaken, he said, "How awesome is this place! This is none other than the **house** of God, and this is the gateway to heaven."

(Genesis 28:17)

וייִרא ויאמר מה נורא המקום הזה אין זה כי אם
בית אלהים וזה שער השמים.

71

32

Hymn

זֶמֶר

Zemer (ZE-mer)

Zemer, Hebrew for "hymn" or "song" appears throughout the Book of Psalms, which could also be described as a book of "hymns" to God. Many of David's lofty and beautiful psalms begin with the word *mizmor*, a form of the word "song." Upon closer observation, however, you'll notice that some psalms begin with the phrase "Of David, a hymn" while others begin with "A hymn, of David." The difference between these two phrases is significant.

When David felt distant from God and wanted to draw closer, he sang to God. The psalm that emerged from that moment of song is recorded in Psalms as "A hymn, of David," for the song preceded, and led to, greater closeness to God. However, if David was already in an elevated spiritual state and sang a song to express his love and devotion to God, the psalm he wrote at that moment is recorded as "Of David, a hymn."

For millennia, the people of Israel have used songs to worship God. In the Tabernacle and Temple, the Levites sang every time a sacrifice was offered on the altar. The beautiful singing of the Levites helped everyone present, and particularly the priests offering the sacrifice, feel the spiritual power of the moment. The songs the Levites sang were taken directly from the Book of Psalms.

One of the most beautiful aspects of the *Shabbat* experience is the tradition of sitting around the table with family and friends and singing *zemirot*, special songs composed to celebrate and honor the seventh day. *Shabbat* is a taste of the time of the Messiah when, as King David says in the Book of Psalms, the entire world will sing to God.

But in the seventh year the land shall have a sabbath of complete rest, a sabbath of God: you shall not sow your field or prune your vineyard. (Leviticus 25:4)

"Of David, a **hymn**.The earth belongs to God and all that it holds, the world and its inhabitants."

(Psalms 24:1)

לדוד מזמור ליהוה הארץ ומלואה תבל וישבי בה.

"It is good to praise God, to **sing hymns** to Your name, O Most High."

(Psalms 92:2)

טוב להודות ליהוה ולזמר לשמך עליון.

33

Israel

יִשְׂרָאֵל

Yisrael (yis-ra-AYL)

Yisrael, Hebrew for Israel, literally means "to wrestle with God." Jacob was given this new name after he wrestled with and overcame an angel of God while returning to the holy land. The Jewish people were originally called *Bnei Yisrael*, the "Children of Israel," for they all descended from one man - Israel, or Jacob.

In Biblical thought, a nation's name is very significant, for it describes the nation's collective character and destiny. Israel's life was full of struggles, from clashes with his brother Esau and his father-in-law Laban to losing his son Joseph and believing he was dead for over twenty years. Nevertheless, Israel never despaired, and his suffering only made him stronger. Israel's character and destiny were passed on to his descendants, the people of Israel, a nation that has faced many terrible struggles throughout its long history yet has managed to not only survive, but thrive.

Though we strive for pure faith in God, the Bible also invites us to "wrestle with God" and to develop a personal and intimate relationship with our Creator that makes space for our questions and our desire to better understand His will in the world. The greatest leaders of Israel "wrestled" with God, including Abraham, who continuously asked God to reconsider his decision to overturn the city of Sodom, and Moses, who told God to erase him from His book if He destroys the nation of Israel because of their sins.

The word *Yisrael* can also be pronounced *yashar li'El*, meaning "straight to God." The struggles we experience in life are meant to bring us closer to God, just as Israel's great struggles and suffering brought him closer to God.

"These are the names of the sons of **Israel** who came to Egypt with Jacob, each coming with his household."

(Exodus 1:1)

ואלה שמות בני **ישראל** הבאים מצרימה את יעקב איש וביתו באו.

"He said, 'Your name shall no longer be Jacob, but **Israel**, for you have striven with beings divine and human, and have prevailed.'"

(Genesis 32:29)

ויאמר לא יעקב יאמר עוד שמך כי אם **ישראל** כי שרית עם אלהים ועם אנשים ותוכל.

34

Justice מִשְׁפָּט

Mishpat (mish-PAT)

The Bible categorizes law into two types, *chukim* and *mishpatim*. *Chukim* are laws that cannot be understood by human reason and logic, such as abstaining from pork and the burning of the red heifer. *Mishpatim* are laws that, though given by God, can be understood through human reason, such as the prohibitions against murder and theft and the obligation to set up courts of law.

The word *shofet*, "judge," derives from the same grammatical root as *mishpatim*. Judges played a central role in the Biblical justice system, serving on three different kinds of courts, each with a different number of judges. A court of 3 judges presided over everyday cases, a court of 23 judges dealt with cases that involved capital punishment and a court of 71 judges was involved with issues that affected the entire nation.

Mishpatim are the backbone of a functioning and flourishing society, so much so that the prophet Isaiah said, "Zion will be redeemed by *mishpat*" (Isaiah 1:27). By building and maintaining a society of justice and lawfulness, the nation of Israel will merit the final redemption.

Interestingly, the Biblical portion immediately following the powerful narrative of the receiving of the Torah on Mount Sinai begins with the verse, "These are the *mishpatim* that you shall set before them" (Exodus 21:1) and then goes on to list many specific and detailed laws. This is the way of the Bible, to juxtapose an elevated spiritual experience with laws that govern the everyday aspects of our lives. The Bible both inspires us to reach out to the Divine and teaches us how to sanctify every mundane moment of our lives.

"You shall appoint **judges** and officers for your tribes, in all the settlements that your God is giving you, and they shall **govern** the people with due **justice**."

(Deuteronomy 16:18)

שפטים ושטרים תתן לך בכל שעריך אשר

יהוה אלהיך נתן לך לשבטיך **ושפטו** את העם

משפט צדק.

"You shall keep My rules and My **laws**, by the pursuit of which human beings shall live: I am God."

(Leviticus 18:5)

ושמרתם את חקתי ואת **משפטי** אשר יעשה

אתם האדם וחי בהם אני יהוה.

35

Kindness

חֶסֶד

Chesed (KHE-sed)

hesed, "kindness," is one of the most fundamental values in Biblical tradition. The Bible begins with an act of *chesed*, when God provided clothing to Adam and Eve after their sin, and ends with an act of *chesed*, when God buried Moses. God's extraordinary *chesed* is emphasized in the Ten Commandments. "But showing kindness to the thousandth generation of those who love Me and keep My commandments." (Exodus 20:6)

The *chasidah*, a non-kosher bird listed in the Bible, has the same root letters as the word *chesed*. Rabbi Shlomo Yitzchaki (1040-1105) writes that this bird is called a *chasidah* because it performs *chesed* by sharing its food with others. But if this is true, asks Rabbi Menachem Mendel of Kotzk (1787-1859), why isn't the righteous *chasidah* bird kosher? He answers that the *chasidah* only shares its food with its own kind, but not with birds of other species. This is not the type of *chesed* that the Bible commands us to exemplify.

Mankind must actively join God, whose "kindness is confirmed forever" (Psalms 89:3), in creating a world filled with *chesed*. Nobody in human history emulated God's *chesed* more than Abraham, who was known for his hospitality towards all people. He and Sarah even designed entrances on all four sides of their tent in order to make it easier and more inviting for people to enter. Abraham's passion for *chesed* was a central reason God chose Abraham to be his vehicle for bringing His word into the world. By teaching monotheism throughout the ancient world, Abraham performed the greatest possible act of *chesed*: bringing people closer to God.

"And showing **kindness** to the thousandth generation of those who love Me and keep My commandments."

(Exodus 20:6)

ועשה **חסד** לאלפים לאהבי ולשמרי מצותי.

"I declare, 'Your **kindness** is confirmed forever; there in the heavens You establish Your faithfulness.'"

(Psalms 89:3)

כי אמרתי עולם **חסד** יבנה שמים תכן אמונתך

בהם.

36

King

Melech (ME-lekh)

Melech, the Hebrew word "king," is used for both human kings and the King of all Kings, God Himself. "God is king for ever and ever; the nations will perish from His land" (Psalms 10:16). Almost every Jewish blessing said over food or for special occasions includes the words *Eloheinu Melech Ha'olam,* meaning "Our God, King of the Universe."

Though the story of Pharaoh, king of Egypt, the first description of a human king in the Bible, is largely negative, God permitted the Israelites to appoint a king to lead the nation. Israelite kings, however, are tasked with a far more exalted role than the average human king. They must serve as God's messengers on Earth, unify the nation of Israel and turn their hearts towards God. Righteous kings like King David and King Hezekiah fulfilled these goals and brought God's glory to the people of Israel.

To ensure they remember their higher mission, Israelite kings are commanded to always carry with them a copy of the Five Books of Moses. Nevertheless, many Biblical kings, such as King Jeroboam and King Menashe, lost sight of their mission and led the people of Israel astray.

In preparation for receiving the Torah at Mount Sinai, God gave the Israelites a lofty goal: to become a *mamlechet kohanim,* a "kingdom of priests." Like the priests who performed the Divine service in the Tabernacle and the Temple and also served as the spiritual teachers of the nation, the Israelites are tasked with bringing the knowledge and awareness of God to the entire world.

"If, after you have entered the land that your God has assigned to you, and taken possession of it and settled in it, you decide, "I will set a **king** over me, like all the nations about me."

(Deuteronomy 17:14)

כי תבא אל הארץ אשר יהוה אלהיך נתן לך
וירשתה וישבתה בה ואמרת אשימה עלי **מלך**
ככל הגוים אשר סביבתי.

"But you shall be to Me a **kingdom** of priests and a holy nation. These are the words that you shall speak to the children of Israel."

(Exodus 19:6)

ואתם תהיו לי **ממלכת** כהנים וגוי קדוש אלה
הדברים אשר תדבר אל בני ישראל.

37

Kingdom מֶמְשָׁלָה

Memshalah (mem-sha-LAH)

Memshalah is used throughout the Bible to refer to a "ruling power" or "kingdom." At the very beginning of Genesis, God created two equally "great lights," the sun and the moon, to rule the day and the night. The Sages explain that the moon complained to God: "Sovereign of the universe! Is it possible for two kings to wear one crown?" God said, "You're right. Go then and make yourself smaller," causing the moon to cease shining its own light and to restrict itself to reflecting the light of the sun.

The children of Israel are also referred to as the "*memshalah* of God," as it says, "Judah became His holy one, Israel, His kingdom" (Psalms 114:2). This reflects the special relationship God established with the children of Israel and that no matter how many external powers try to rule over them, they are always and forever ruled by God alone.

Maimonides, the great medieval rabbi, wrote that "In the future, the Messianic king will arise and renew the Davidic dynasty, restoring it to its initial *memshalah*." This will come together with the ingathering of all of the Jewish exiles and the rebuilding of the Temple in Jerusalem.

In the modern State of Israel, the government is called the *Memshalah* and the Prime Minister is referred to as the *Rosh HaMemshalah*, the "Head of the Government." In modern Israel, we are blessed to witness the rebirth of Hebrew as a spoken language, an essential aspect of the Jewish people's return to Israel and the establishment of their own, independent *memshalah*.

"God made the two great lights, the greater light to **rule** the day and the lesser light to **rule** the night, and the stars."

(Genesis 1:16)

ויעש אלהים את שני המארת הגדלים את המאור הגדל **לממשלת** היום ואת המאור הקטן **לממשלת** הלילה ואת הכוכבים.

"Judah became His holy one, Israel, His **kingdom**."

(Psalms 114:2)

היתה יהודה לקדשו ישראל **ממשלותיו.**

38

Land

Eretz (E-retz)

אֶרֶץ

"**I**n the beginning God created the heavens and the earth (*eretz*)" (Genesis 1:1). After briefly mentioning the creation of the heavens, the rest of the Bible is focused squarely on Earth, where God placed human beings and enjoined us to follow His word and carry out His will. "The heavens belong to God, but the land He gave over to man" (Psalms 115:16). Our mission in life is to make this physical world a Godly world!

But the Bible is particularly focused on one specific area of land: the land of Israel.

God's first words to Abraham were "Go forth from your native land and from your father's house to the land that I will show you" (Genesis 12:1). Only in Israel would Abraham be able to carry out his mission to bring the knowledge and light of God to the world. And only in Israel will Abraham's descendants complete his holy mission and bring the final redemption.

The nation of Israel, the land of Israel and God Himself are intimately and eternally bound to one another. "It is a land which God looks after, on which God always keeps His eye, from the year's beginning to the year's end" (Deuteronomy 11:12). While God created and cares for the entire world, His presence in the land of Israel is palpable. Countless visitors and pilgrims to Israel, from ancient times until today, testify to experiencing a powerful closeness to God unlike anywhere else in the world.

"God said to Abram, "Go forth from your native **land** and from your father's house to the **land** that I will show you."

(Genesis 12:1)

ויאמר יהוה אל אברם לך לך **מארצך** וממולדתך ומבית אביך אל **הארץ** אשר אראך.

"The heavens belong to God, but the **land** He gave over to man."

(Psalms 115:16)

השמים שמים ליהוה **והארץ** נתן לבני אדם.

39

Law

הֲלָכָה

Halacha (ha-la-KHAH)

The Hebrew word *halacha* derives from the word *holech*, "to walk," and is most commonly used to refer to the Jewish tradition's large body of commandments and laws. This linguistic connection reflects the purpose of Jewish law: to teach us how to "walk" in God's ways through this world.

A teaching from the Talmud illustrates this idea. "One who studies *Halachot* (Torah laws) every day is assured of a place in the World to Come. The verse in Habakkuk says: '*The ways of the world (Halichot) are His*' (Habakkuk 3:6). The Rabbis explain: Do not read '*Halichot*,' meaning 'ways of the world,' but rather "*Halachot*," meaning the 'laws of the Torah.'"

"The ways of the world" are the mundane, everyday things we do throughout each day of our lives, from the time we wake up in the morning until we go to sleep at night, like getting dressed in the morning, eating breakfast and commuting to work. The Sages teach us that the laws of the Torah that direct our everyday lives are meant to align these mundane parts of our lives with God's ways. They provide us with constant opportunities to bring God-consciousness into our daily lives and infuse holiness into the mundane.

This is what Jethro was referring to when he said to his son-in-law Moses, "Enjoin upon them the laws and the teachings, and make known to them the way they are to go and the practices they are to follow" (Exodus 18:20). The laws of the Bible show us the path on which we should walk and, as a result, help us to follow the ways of God, uplifting and sanctifying our lives with great purpose and meaning.

"Enjoin upon them the laws and the teachings, and make known to them the way they are **to go** and the practices they are to follow."

(Exodus 18:20)

והזהרתה אתהם את החקים ואת
התורת והודעת להם את הדרך **ילכו** בה ואת
המעשה אשר יעשון.

"When He stands, He makes the earth shake; when He glances, He makes nations tremble. The age-old mountains are shattered, the primeval hills sink low. The **ways** of the world are His."

(Habakkuk 3:6)

עמד וימדד ארץ ראה ויתר גוים ויתפצצו הררי
עד שחו גבעות עולם **הליכות** עולם לו.

40

Life

Chayim (kha-YEEM)

חַיִּים

"L'*chayim!*" is the well known toast that Jews make to celebrate special life moments and milestones. It means "to life!"

The entire Bible can be summed up in this one word, as its overarching value is the respect for and sanctity of life. For by respecting the lives of others, we respect the God Who created everything. In other words, if we truly respect God, we will naturally respect all other living things. "I have put before you life and death...choose life" (Deuteronomy 30:15,19).

Despite the great importance of each and every one of the Bible's 613 commandments, one is permitted, even obligated, to violate almost any commandment in order to save a life. One is obligated to violate the laws of *Shabbat* or the *kosher* laws if one's life, or someone else's life, is at risk. The value of life is supreme.

Not only is following God's will and word the best way to live one's life, it is the only way of life that is truly considered "living." The Talmud teaches that evil people are considered as if they are dead even while they are still alive, while righteous people are considered alive, even after they have left this world.

The Bible also uses the word *chayim* in regard to purification rituals for those who have become impure. Whether the impurity derives from a skin affliction or contact with a dead body, "living waters" that come from natural sources like rivers, springs and rainfall are required for the ritual to have its intended effect. Life is the source of purity.

"I call heaven and earth to witness against you this day: I have put before you **life** and death, blessing and curse. Choose life - if you and your offspring would **live**."

(Deuteronomy 30:19)

העדתי בכם היום את השמים ואת הארץ
החיים והמות נתתי לפניך הברכה והקללה
ובחרת **בחיים** למען **תחיה** אתה וזרעך.

"Isaac's servants, digging in the wadi, found there a well of **living** waters."

(Genesis 26:19)

ויחפרו עבדי יצחק בנחל וימצאו שם באר מים
חיים.

89

41

Listen

Shemah (sh'-MA)

Shemah, Hebrew for "listen," is the first word of Judaism's most important and foundational prayer, "Listen, Israel! The Lord is our God, God is One" (Deuteronomy 6:4), which declares our faith in the one and only God. The Bible commands us to recite the *Shemah* every morning and evening: "And these words, which I command you this day, shall be upon your heart... and you shall speak of them... when you lie down and when you get up" (Deuteronomy 6:6-7). By reciting the *Shemah* prayer each day and night, we do not forget its powerful message.

Rabbi Akiva was the leading rabbi of Israel during the 2nd century CE, a time of terrible Roman persecution. Among other rabbis, he was arrested by the Romans and tortured to death for teaching the Bible in public. As the Romans burned him to death, he cried out the words of the *Shemah*. His students cried out, "Master, at a time like this you can say the *Shemah*?" Rabbi Akiva responded, "All of my life I have strived to fulfill the verse 'You shall love God with all your heart and all of your soul.' Now I finally have the chance to do so." With the words of the *Shemah* on his lips, his soul left the world. Rabbi Akiva's act of spiritual bravery is the source for the Jewish practice of reciting the *Shemah* before death. Untold numbers of Jews recited the *Shemah* in their final moments before being murdered by Nazis during the Holocaust.

Upon receiving the Torah, the children of Israel proclaimed "we will do and we will listen," committing themselves to live according to God's word as written in the Bible, even before they heard what was written in it, an extraordinary commitment of faith.

"**Listen**, Israel! Hashem is our God, Hashem is One."

(Deuteronomy 6:4)

שמע ישראל יהוה אלהינו יהוה אחד.

"Then he took the record of the covenant and read it aloud to the people. And they said, 'All that God has spoken we will do and we will **listen**!'"

(Exodus 24:7)

ויקח ספר הברית ויקרא באזני העם ויאמרו כל

אשר דבר יהוה נעשה ונשמע.

42

Love

אַהֲבָה

Ahavah (a-ha-VAH)

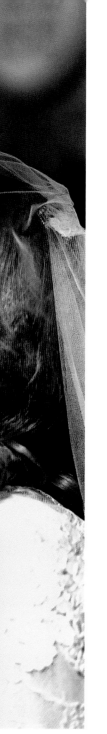

I n our relationship with God and in our relationship with others, the Bible tells us to *love*. But what does it really mean to love?

The Hebrew word for love, *ahava,* contains the root word *hav,* which means "to give."

According to the Bible, loving and giving are deeply intertwined. Superficially, people believe that we *give* to those we *love*. But the truth is actually the opposite: we *love* the people we *give* to. The act of giving creates closeness, connection and love.

In our relationships with others, God wants us to be givers, not takers. We are meant to emulate God Himself, to share and provide others with what they need rather than trying to take what we can from them.

The Bible also commands us to love the stranger: "Love the stranger, for you were strangers in the land of Egypt" (Deuteronomy 10:19). How can we find the motivation to love and give to someone who is a stranger? We must believe, in the depths of our hearts, that every human being is created "in the image of God." That alone is reason enough to love the stranger.

Finally, God wants the same thing in our relationship with Him. He wants us to love Him! But how can we give to God when He lacks nothing and needs nothing from us? We study His word, strive to fulfill His word in our lives and work to build a world that is based on His word.

"You shall **love** Hashem your God with all your heart and with all your soul and with all your might."

(Deuteronomy 6:5)

ואהבת את יהוה אלהיך בכל לבבך ובכל נפשך ובכל מאדך.

"You shall not take vengeance or bear a grudge against members of your people. **Love** your fellow as yourself: I am God."

(Leviticus 19:18)

לא תקם ולא תטר את בני עמך ואהבת לרעך כמוך אני יהוה.

43

PHOTO: HANOVEL

Man

Adam (Ah-dam)

אָדָם

In the creation story at the beginning of Genesis, G-d did not assign names to the animals. Only human beings are named, as it is written, "Let us make man (*Adam*)" (Genesis 1:26). What does this name mean, and what does it teach us about the uniqueness of humanity?

The Hebrew word *Adam* shares the same root as adama, the Hebrew word for "earth." The Bible teaches that the first human was made "from the earth," as it is written, "And the Lord God formed man of dust from the earth" (Genesis 2:7).

Man, however, was not the only creature formed from the earth. Superficially, man and animal appear to be fundamentally the same, as both were formed from the *adama*. "God said, "Let the earth bring forth every kind of living creature" (Genesis 1:24). But there is more to mankind than earth!

Adam was created "in the image of God" (Genesis 1:27), and "blew into his nostrils the breath of life" (Genesis 2:7). Though our bodies come from the same earth as the animals, God created us with a higher level of soul and a loftier purpose.

Though the name *Adam* is linked to *adama* (earth), it is also linked to an entirely different word, *edameh*, meaning "I will be like." As the verse in Isaiah states: "I will ascend above the heights of the clouds; *I will be like (edameh)* the Most High!" (Isaiah 14:14).

Mankind, *Adam*, must choose. We can choose to act like animals and be people of physicality, of the earth (*adama*). Or we can choose to control our desires and to emulate God and His holy ways (*edameh*). The choice is ours.

"And God said, "Let us make **man** in our image, after our likeness. They shall rule the fish of the sea, the birds of the sky, the cattle, the whole earth, and all the creeping things that creep on earth."

(Genesis 1:26)

ויאמר אלהים נעשה **אדם** בצלמנו כדמותנו
וירדו בדגת הים ובעוף השמים ובבהמה ובכל
הארץ ובכל הרמש הרמש על הארץ.

"God formed the **man** from the **earth**, blowing into his nostrils the breath of life: the man became a living being."

(Genesis 2:7)

וייצר יהוה אלהים את **האדם** עפר מן **האדמה**
ויפח באפיו נשמת חיים ויהי האדם לנפש חיה.

44

Mercy

רַחֲמִים

Rachamim (ra-kha-MEEM)

I n traditional Jewish prayer, God is often referred to as *Av HaRachaman*, "Father of Mercy," for mercy is one of His most central attributes. After the terrible sin of the golden calf, Moses returned to Mount Sinai and pleaded with God to forgive His people. After his prayers were accepted, Moses took advantage of this opportune moment and asked God to provide the people of Israel with a way to access His mercy should they fall into sin again in the future. God responded by sharing the secret of the 13 Attributes of Mercy (Exodus 34:6-7). These 13 Attributes are recited by Jews during the holiest moments of the year and form the basis of the holy prayers recited on Yom Kippur, the Day of Atonement.

The Talmud states that one who is not merciful is not considered part of the Israelite nation, for mercy is part of the chosen nation's "spiritual DNA." Only a merciful people can be the messengers who bring God's word to humanity. "Keep the commandments of Hashem your God and walk in His ways" (Deuteronomy 28:9). The Sages explain that we are commanded to emulate God in our lives: "Just as God is merciful, so must you be merciful."

Rechem, the Hebrew word for "womb," is linguistically related to *rachamim*. A fetus in the womb receives everything it needs to grow and to prepare for life in the outside world. The baby's mother constantly gives of herself for the sake of the life inside of her, making the womb a place of unceasing love and mercy.

"God is good to all, and His **mercy** is upon all His works."

(Psalms 145:9)

טוב יהוה לכל ו**רחמיו** על כל מעשיו.

"Thus said God, Lord of Hosts: Execute true justice; deal loyally and **mercifully** with one another."

(Zechariah 7:9)

כה אמר יהוה צבאות לאמר משפט אמת שפטו
וחסד ו**רחמים** עשו איש את אחיו.

97

45

Messiah מָשִׁיחַ

Mashiach (ma-SHEE-akh)

Mashiach, Hebrew for "Messiah," literally means "the anointed one," for the Messiah will one day be the king of Israel and will be anointed with oil, as kings were once anointed in ancient Israel. Like his father David, Solomon was anointed when he became king, as it says, "The priest Zadok took the horn of oil from the Tent and anointed Solomon. They sounded the horn and all the people shouted, 'Long live King Solomon!'" (1 Kings 1:39).

The oil used to anoint kings in ancient times was also used to anoint the high priests who served in the holy Temple in Jerusalem. Oil represents wisdom and is meant as a blessing for the nation's leaders to serve righteously and according to the wisdom they receive from God.

The vessels of the Tabernacle were also anointed with oil, consecrating them and transforming them into something sacred to be used to serve and worship God.

Jewish tradition teaches that the original oil that was used to anoint kings and priests in ancient Israel still exists, though it is hidden. At the end of days, it will be revealed and used to anoint the King Messiah and the High Priest in the rebuilt Third Temple. This will be a fulfillment of the verse, "Take us back, God, to Yourself, and let us come back; renew our days as of old!" (Lamentations 5:21). At that time, leaders from all over the world will come to Jerusalem to learn from the *Mashiach* how to govern and lead their people in the ways of God.

"The priest Zadok took the horn of oil from the Tent and anointed Solomon. They sounded the horn and all the people shouted, 'Long live King Solomon!'"

(1 Kings 1:39)

ויקח צדוק הכהן את קרן השמן מן האהל **וימשח** את שלמה ויתקעו בשופר ויאמרו כל העם יחי המלך שלמה.

"And the anointed priest shall take some of the bull's blood and bring it into the Tent of Meeting."

(Leviticus 4:5)

ולקח הכהן **המשיח** מדם הפר והביא אתו אל אהל מועד.

46

New

חָדָשׁ

Chadash (kha-DASH)

Chadash, meaning "new," is most commonly found in the Bible in the form *chodesh*, meaning "month."

God's very first commandment to the people of Israel was the consecration of the months. "This month shall mark for you the beginning of the months; it shall be the first of the months of the year for you" (Exodus 12:2). The first day of each month is known as *Rosh Chodesh*, literally "the head of the month," and it is a special day dedicated to repentance and joy. In the Temple in Jerusalem, extra sacrifices were brought on the first day of every month to express this sentiment.

The Hebrew calendar is primarily a lunar calendar. After the moon has all but disappeared from the night sky, it reappears, marking the beginning of a new month. The constant waning and waxing of the moon teaches us that we can always start again. No matter our failures or what we have been through, we can begin anew.

Renewal is essential to serving God. "Sing to God a new song" (Psalms 96:1). King David encourages us to constantly strive for new ways to serve God. The "old songs" we have sung for God are beautiful, but we must never stop composing new songs of service for God!

Eventually this will bring a new and brighter era for humanity, when the whole world will be cognizant of God's presence, as it says in the Jewish prayer book: "A new light will shine upon Zion."

"This **month** shall mark for you the beginning of the **months**; it shall be the first of the **months** of the year for you."

(Exodus 12:2)

החדש הזה לכם ראש חדשים ראשון הוא לכם
לחדשי השנה.

"Sing to God a **new** song, sing to God all of the earth."

(Psalms 96:1)

שירו ליהוה שיר חדש שירו ליהוה כל הארץ.

47

One

אֶחָד

Echad (e-KHAD)

Echad, "one," appears in one of the most powerful verses in all of the Bible: "Hear, O Israel! *Hashem* is our God, *Hashem* is one" (Deuteronomy 6:4). This verse succinctly expresses our faith in one God, and so we are commanded to recite it twice each day, once in the morning and once at night.

The Hebrew word *achdut*, "unity," is based on the word *echad*. The Sages teach that when the children of Israel stood at the bottom of Mount Sinai they achieved extraordinary *achdut*, joining together "like one person with one heart." In the merit of this unity, they received the Bible from God.

Unity, however, can also be used for negative purposes. At the beginning of the story of the Tower of Babel, we read "Everyone on earth had the same language and the same words" (Genesis 11:1). Commendably, the people of that generation joined together as one, but then tragically worked together to rebel against their Creator. Mankind must unite, but only to perform God's will.

Echad also appears in the Bible's description of the building of the Tabernacle. After the people brought all the necessary materials and constructed the many parts of the building, God commanded them to weave huge pieces of cloth to surround the Tabernacle from all sides in order that the "Tabernacle becomes one." This is not merely a technical description of the structure of the Tabernacle. The Tabernacle was a microcosm of God's world. By binding the Tabernacle together so it became one, the children of Israel symbolically affirmed God's oneness and unity in the world.

"Hear, O Israel! *Hashem* is our God, *Hashem* is **one**."

(Deuteronomy 6:4)

שמע ישראל יהוה אלהינו יהוה **אחד.**

"And make fifty gold clasps, and couple the cloths to one another with the clasps, so that the Tabernacle becomes **one**."

(Exodus 26:6)

ועשית חמשים קרסי זהב וחברת את היריעת
אשה אל אחתה בקרסים והיה המשכן **אחד.**

48

Passover

פֶּסַח

Pesach (PE-sakh)

Pesach, Hebrew for "Passover," first appears in the verse that describes God "passing over" the houses of the Israelites during the tenth and final plague, the killing of the firstborn. In order to save themselves, the Israelites were commanded to take the blood of a slaughtered sheep and place it on the door post of their home. This served as a sign that Israelites lived in the house, preventing the destroyer from entering the home and killing the firstborn of the family during the plague. In recognition of this miracle, the foundational holiday of the people of Israel is called "Passover."

When the Temple stood in Jerusalem, the people of Israel were obligated to celebrate the three pilgrimage festivals - Passover, Shavuot and Sukkot - together with God in the holy city. "Three times a year... [you] shall appear before your God in the place that God will choose" (Deuteronomy 16:16). On the afternoon before Passover began, each family would bring the *korban pesach*, the sacrificial paschal lamb, which was eaten at the Passover *Seder*.

The word *pesach* is derived from a combination of two other Hebrew words, *peh* and *sach*, meaning "the mouth speaks." This reflects an essential element of *Seder* night, the first night of Passover, when Jews are commanded to *speak* about the miracles that God performed for their ancestors in Egypt. Every year, parents are obligated to share this story with their children to ensure the tradition and history of the people of Israel is passed on to each successive generation. On this night, we remember God's great love for the Israelites and the awesome wonders and miracles He performed to bring the chosen nation from slavery to freedom.

"For God, when going through to smite the Egyptians, will see the blood on the lintel and the two doorposts, and God will **pass over** the door and not let the destroyer enter and smite your home."

(Exodus 12:23)

ועבר יהוה לנגף את מצרים וראה את הדם על המשקוף ועל שתי המזוזת **ופסח** יהוה על הפתח ולא יתן המשחית לבא אל בתיכם לנגף.

"Observe the month of Spring and offer a **passover** sacrifice to your God, for it was in the month of Spring, at night, that your God freed you from Egypt."

(Deuteronomy 16:1)

שמור את חדש האביב ועשית **פסח** ליהוה אלהיך כי בחדש האביב הוציאך יהוה אלהיך ממצרים לילה.

49

Peace

שָׁלוֹם

Shalom (sha-LOM)

Shalom, Hebrew for "peace," is so central to Biblical values that the Sages teach *Shalom* is one of God's names. In Jewish thought, peace is not merely the absence of war, but rather a harmonious integration of different perspectives and attitudes, in which each view finds its place and is properly appreciated as part of a greater whole. For this reason, *shalom* is derived from the Hebrew word *shalem*, meaning "whole."

"Her ways are pleasant ways, and all her paths are peaceful" (Proverbs 3:17). Every commandment, teaching and detail of the Bible is dedicated to bringing true peace to the world. As the Sages say, "God has not found a vessel which contains blessing for Israel but peace." Only when and where there is peace can God's blessings truly manifest.

When the Temple stood in Jerusalem, the priests blessed the nation every day with the priestly blessing (Numbers 6:24-26). The last of these blessings states "May God bestow favor upon you and grant you peace!" Every Friday night at the *Shabbat* dinner table, Jewish parents use these very same verses to bless their children. The loftiest blessing we can bestow upon our children is peace.

"God will grant strength to His people; God will bless His people with peace" (Psalms 29:11). God's ultimate goal is to bestow peace upon His chosen people, but the path to peace is neither simple nor easy. When confronted with external enemies, the people of Israel must possess and wield strength until its enemies are subdued. This is the goal of the Israel Defense Forces, whose mission is "to preserve the State of Israel, to protect its independence, and to foil attempts by its enemies to disrupt the normal life within it." With strength we can achieve peace.

"Her ways are pleasant ways, and all her paths are **peaceful**."

(Proverbs 3:17)

דרכיה דרכי נעם וכל נתיבותיה **שלום**.

"God will grant strength to His people; God will bless His people with **peace**."

(Psalms 29:11)

יהוה עז לעמו יתן יהוה יברך את עמו **בשלום**.

Portion

נַחֲלָה

Nachalah (na-kha-LAH)

Upon the completion of the Israelite's conquest of the land of Israel, the land was divided up into twelve *nachalot*, twelve "portions," one for each tribe. Levi, the only tribe that did not receive a particular portion like the others, was scattered among the lands of the other tribes, in 48 different Levite cities. The Levites subsisted on agricultural tithes that the other tribes were obligated to give them from the produce of their fields. This freed the Levites to perform their designated duties in the Temple in Jerusalem and to serve as religious teachers for the nation.

The children of Israel are referred to in the Bible as "God's portion." "But God took you and brought you out of Egypt... to be God's very own portion" (Deuteronomy 4:20). God did not free the Israelites from their slavery in Egypt simply to become an independent nation like many other nations in the world. Rather, He took the people of Israel to make them His chosen nation, a nation that would bring the light of God to the world. God said to Moses, "Go to Pharaoh and say to him, 'Thus says the God of the Hebrews: Let My people go to worship Me'" (Exodus 9:1). The people of Israel must be free in order to worship God.

The grammatical root of *nachalah* is *nachal*, meaning "stream." Though the land of Israel does not have many lakes, it was blessed with many flowing streams, as it says in the verse, "For your God is bringing you into a good land, a land with streams and springs and fountains issuing from plain and hill" (Deuteronomy 8:7).

"The levitical priests, the whole tribe of Levi, shall have no territorial **portion** with Israel. They shall live only off God's offerings by fire as their **portion**."

(Deuteronomy 18:1)

לא יהיה לכהנים הלוים כל *שבט* לוי חלק **ונחלה** עם ישראל אשי יהוה **ונחלתו** יאכלון.

"But God took you and brought you out of Egypt, that iron blast furnace, to be God's very own **portion,** as is now the case."

(Deuteronomy 4:20)

ואתכם לקח יהוה ויצא אתכם מכור הברזל ממצרים להיות לו לעם **נחלה** כיום הזה.

51

Praise

Hallel (*ha-LAYL*)

הַלֵּל

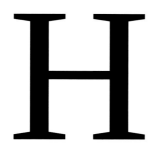

Hallel, the Hebrew word for "praise," is the linguistic root of the most common word used in the worship of God by people around the world: *Hallelujah*!

In Judaism there is a special collection of Psalms (113-118) that collectively are called *Hallel*. The *Hallel* Psalms are sung in joyous fashion on special holidays such as Passover, Sukkot, and Hanukkah.

The primary goal of *Hallel* is recognizing God's ability to override the laws of nature and perform miracles and acts of salvation on our behalf. Although we are meant to view every phenomenon in nature - from the flowering of a rose to the rainfall that gives life to the land - as an act of God, it's easy to become used to nature and forget that God is the hidden Mover behind it all. And so God, on occasion, performs miracles to remind us of the truth that all of nature is really in His hands. The Baal Shem Tov, the great 18th century founder of the Hasidic movement, taught that if we would understand that every moment we are alive is indeed a miracle, we would praise God all day long, everyday.

By praising God, we recognize the goodness that is in the world and in our own lives. Focusing on the good enables us to banish any sense of despair or worry. As modern psychology teaches, being positive and seeing the good breeds more positivity and goodness in a person's life.

In his Book of Psalms, King David taught us how to open our hearts and truly praise God with all of our being. It's fitting that the last of the 150 psalms ends with the verse, "Let everything that has breath praise God, *Hallelujah*!" (Psalms 150:6).

"Let everything that has breath **praise** God, *Hallelujah*!"

(Psalms 150:6)

כל הנשמה תהלל יה **הללויה.**

"Every day I will bless You and **praise** Your name forever and ever."

(Psalms 145:2)

בכל יום אברכך **ואהללה** שמך לעולם ועד.

52

Redemption גְּאוּלָה

Geulah (g'-u-LAH)

Geulah, Hebrew for "redemption," is often used in Jewish liturgy to refer to the future Messianic age. It expresses the fundamental Jewish belief that the problems of our world and the ills of human society will one day cease to exist and belief in God and knowledge of God will spread throughout the world.

The Talmud compares *geulah* to the morning dawn and rising of the sun. At first, it is a very slow process and one may not notice that the darkness is turning into light. Eventually, though, the light shines more and more powerfully, until it is apparent to all that the morning has come.

The first *geulah* mentioned in the Bible was God's promise to free the Israelites from their bondage in Egypt, as it says, "I will redeem you with an outstretched arm" (Exodus 6:6). This promise extends to future generations as well, promising that all future periods of oppression will eventually end as well. As the prophet Isaiah says, "He shall come as redeemer to Zion, to those in Jacob who turn back from sin, declares Hashem" (59:20).

The Bible frequently uses the word *geulah* to refer to the redemption of lands that are sold by its owner, often to pay off a debt. The person in debt, or their family member or friend, is only permitted to redeem the land within a certain time period. With the Jubilee year, however, all lands were returned to their original owners by force of Biblical law, which demonstrated that ownership of land is ultimately determined by God.

"Say, therefore, to the Israelite people: 'I am God. I will free you from the labors of the Egyptians and deliver you from their bondage. I will **redeem** you with an outstretched arm and through extraordinary chastisements.'"

(Exodus 6:6)

לכן אמר לבני ישראל אני יהוה והוצאתי אתכם
מתחת סבלת מצרים והצלתי אתכם מעבדתם
וגאלתי אתכם בזרוע נטויה ובשפטים גדלים.

"If any party sells a dwelling house in a walled city, it may be **redeemed** until a year has elapsed since its sale; the **redemption** period shall be a year."

(Leviticus 25:29)

ואיש כי ימכר בית מושב עיר חומה והיתה
גאלתו עד תם שנת ממכרו ימים תהיה **גאלתו.**

53

Remember

Zachor (za-KHOR)

זָכוֹר

God commonly uses the word *zachor*, Hebrew for "remember," when instructing the children of Israel to remain aware of something of great importance. When God commands us to "Remember the Sabbath day, to keep it holy" (Exodus 20:7), it means that the holiness of the Sabbath is meant to permeate our entire week as we anticipate and yearn for the opportunity to draw closer to God on His holy day of rest.

Moses commands us to "Remember this day, when you came out from Egypt" (Exodus 13:3). By remembering the Exodus, we recall God's incredible love for the Israelites in freeing them from their bondage as well as our responsibility to care for the oppressed and downtrodden of the world.

"Remember what Amalek did to you on your journey..." (Deuteronomy 25:17). This remembrance is accompanied by a commandment to destroy Amalek, as the prophet Samuel ordered Saul to do, but which Saul failed to do completely, allowing the seed of Amalek to continue.

In Jewish liturgy, we ask God to remember that we are the descendants of Abraham, Isaac and Jacob in order to invoke the merit of the patriarchs chosen by God to bring His word into the world. Moses asks God to remember this merit after God grew angry at His people and threatened to destroy them.

The Jewish New Year, *Rosh Hashanah*, is referred to as *Yom Ha'Zikaron*, "The Day of Remembrance," for Adam, the first human being, was created on this day. Fittingly, we dedicate this day to remember God's purpose in creating us and how we are meant to live our lives.

"**Remember** what Amalek did to you on your journey, after you left Egypt."

(Deuteronomy 25:17)

זכור את אשר עשה לך עמלק בדרך בצאתכם ממצרים.

"**Remember** Your servants, Abraham, Isaac, and Israel, how You swore to them by Yourself and said to them: I will make your offspring as numerous as the stars of heaven, and I will give to your offspring this whole land of which I spoke, to possess forever."

(Exodus 32:13)

זכר לאברהם ליצחק ולישראל עבדיך אשר נשבעת להם בך ותדבר אלהם ארבה את זרעכם ככוכבי השמים וכל הארץ הזאת אשר אמרתי אתן לזרעכם ונחלו לעלם.

54

Repentance תְּשׁוּבָה
Teshuvah (t'-shu-VAH)

Teshuvah, Hebrew for "repentance," comprises a critical aspect of our relationship with God. God knows that we are imperfect beings and understands that sometimes we fail and fall. We all have shortcomings and urges that lead us astray. But when we sin, all is not lost, for we have been given the great gift of *teshuvah*, the opportunity to repent. Tellingly, the word *teshuvah* also means "return," for repentance is much more than regretting our sins or the promise to be better. *Teshuvah* is the return to God and to our true and holy selves.

This spiritual return has the unique ability to overturn God's decrees. "God saw what they did, how they were repenting from their evil ways. And God renounced the punishment He had planned to bring upon them, and did not carry it out" (Jonah 3:10). God loves humanity and does not want to punish us, and so He gives us many chances to repent before a punishment is actually carried out.

The letters of the word *teshuvah*, when rearranged, spell the word *busha*, meaning "embarrassment." When we are truly embarrassed for having committed a sin, we are inspired to return to God and His ways.

The modern day return of the Jewish people to Israel is a national form of *teshuvah*, as the prophet Jeremiah said, "Your children shall return to their country" (31:17). Though the Jewish people have not yet completed their spiritual repentance, their physical return to the land of Israel is an essential part of this historical redemptive process.

"**Return** us, God, to You and we will **return**; renew our days as of old!"

(Lamentations 5:21)

השיבנו יהוה אליך ונשובה חדש ימינו כקדם.

"God saw what they did, how they were **repenting** from their evil ways. And God renounced the punishment He had planned to bring upon them, and did not carry it out."

(Jonah 3:10)

וירא האלהים את מעשיהם כי שבו מדרכם הרעה וינחם האלהים על הרעה אשר דבר לעשות להם ולא עשה.

55

Rest

מְנוּחָה

Menuchah (m'-nu-KHAH)

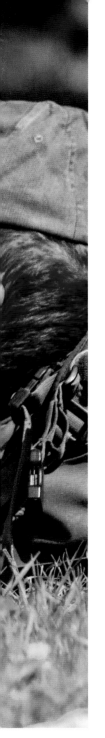

Menuchah, Hebrew for "rest," is often used in the Bible to describe how God rested after the six days of creation. This established the seventh day, *Shabbat*, as a day of rest for all time, both to honor God as the Creator of all things and to provide humanity with a day to reflect upon the purpose of our existence in this world.

The Bible also uses *menuchah* to refer to the Land of Israel, where the people of Israel would settle and "rest" and finally become a nation in their own land. As the verse states, "Because you have not yet come to the allotted rest and inheritance that your God is giving you" (Deuteronomy 12:9).

Rashi, the great Bible commentator, writes that *menuchah* specifically refers to Shiloh, the longtime home of the Tabernacle in Israel and the spiritual center of the 12 tribes of Israel before King Solomon built the first Temple in Jerusalem. *Menuchah* is a fitting word for the site of the Tabernacle, for the primary purpose of the Tabernacle was to create a physical space for God's presence to "rest" in the midst of the people of Israel and all of humanity.

In one of his most well-known psalms, King David uses *menuchah* to describe the rest and tranquility that only God can provide to humanity. "He makes me lie down in green pastures; He leads me to water in places of *repose*" (Psalm 23:2). God is our constant source of support; only through our relationship with Him can we experience rest and tranquility, and realize that we lack nothing.

"For in six days God made heaven and earth and sea—and all that is in them—and then **rested** on the seventh day; therefore God blessed the Shabbat day and hallowed it.

(Exodus 20:11)

כי *ששת* ימים עשה יהוה את השמים ואת הארץ את הים ואת כל אשר בם **וינח** ביום השביעי על כן ברך יהוה את יום השבת ויקדשהו.

"Because you have not yet come to the allotted **rest** and inheritance that Hashem your God is giving you."

(Deuteronomy 12:9)

כי לא באתם עד עתה אל **המנוחה** ואל הנחלה אשר יהוה אלהיך נתן לך.

56

Sabbath

Shabbat (sha-BAT)

שַׁבָּת

Shabbat, Hebrew for "Sabbath," derives from the Hebrew word *lishbot*, "to rest." It is the name given to the seventh day of creation, when God rested after creating the world in six days. At Mount Sinai, God commanded the Israelites to rest on this day as well.

The word *Shabbat* is also related to the Hebrew word *la'shevet*, meaning "to sit" or "to dwell." The act of settling the land of Israel is called *yishuv ha'aretz*, and communities in the land of Israel are often called *yishuvim*, literally "dwellings." Along the same lines, a school for Bible study is called a *yeshiva* in Hebrew, because students and scholars sit around tables, probing and exploring the wisdom of God found in the Bible and other sacred texts.

Shabbat is also connected to the Hebrew word *la'shuv*, "to return," a word often used to connote repentance and returning to God, as it says in the Book of Lamentations, "Return us, God, to You, and let us come back; renew our days as of old!" (Lamentations 5:21). *Shabbat* is not only a day of physical rest but is also a day of returning to our true spiritual selves and realigning our lives with God's will. Our physical rest on *Shabbat* creates the time and space to contemplate, study and bask in the joy of God's presence.

The Sages refer to *Shabbat* as a great gift from God. In our generation, this gift is perhaps more precious than ever before. *Shabbat* offers us a respite from our culture's obsession with productivity and from the overwhelming and constant presence of technology. A day of freedom from all mundane concerns, *Shabbat* is a weekly opportunity to reconnect with God, our loved ones, and the things that truly matter.

"Remember the **Sabbath** day and keep it holy."

(Exodus 20:8)

זכור את יום **השבת** לקדשו.

"Impress them upon your children. Recite them when you **sit** at home and when you are away, when you lie down and when you get up."

(Deuteronomy 6:7)

ושננתם לבניך ודברת בם **בשבתך** בביתך
ובלכתך בדרך ובשכבך ובקומך.

57

Sacrifice

Korban (kor-BAN)

קָרְבָּן

Korban, or "sacrifice" in Hebrew, usually refers to the animal sacrifices described at length in the Book of Leviticus and which were a central aspect of the Temple service.

In modern times, many people struggle to understand why God commanded us to bring animal sacrifices, but considering the linguistic root of the word *korban* can help. The word *korban* derives from the Hebrew word *karov*, meaning "close." The purpose of the korbanot is to help us grow closer to God.

In the ancient Temple, the Israelites brought many kinds of sacrifices, including sin offerings, thanksgiving offerings and, communal offerings. Some were burned completely on the altar, some were partially eaten by the priests and others were also eaten by the people who brought them. The main goal of all the sacrifices was to help people feel closer to God.

Sacrifices were a tool to inspire us to experience various emotions, such as regret for wrongdoing or gratitude for the miracles and blessings in our lives. Ultimately, God desires our hearts and our obedience. Sacrificing something of value and bringing it as an offering to God is a powerful way to facilitate that experience.

The prophet Isaiah rebuked the Israelites for carrying out the sacrificial rituals in the Temple but not adhering to the Biblical values that create a just society. After crying out, "What need have I of all your sacrifices?" he adds, "Wash yourselves clean; put your evil doings away from My sight, cease to do evil" (Isaiah 1:16). Though sacrifices play an important role in our worship of God, they are ultimately a means to a more important end.

"Speak to the people of Israel and say to them: When any of you presents a **sacrifice** of cattle to God, you shall choose your **offering** from the herd or from the flock."

(Leviticus 1:2)

דבר אל בני ישראל ואמרת אלהם אדם כי
יקריב מכם **קרבן** ליהוה מן הבהמה מן הבקר
ומן הצאן **תקריבו** את קרבנכם.

"'What need have I of all your **sacrifices**?' says Hashem. 'I am sated with burnt offerings of rams, and suet of fatlings, and blood of bulls; and I have no delight in lambs and he-goats.'"

(Isaiah 1:11)

למה לי רב זבחיכם יאמר יהוה שבעתי עלות
אילים וחלב מריאים ודם פרים וכבשים
ועתודים לא חפצתי.

58

PHOTO: LAURA BEN DAVID

Service

עֲבוֹדָה

Avodah (a-vo-DAH)

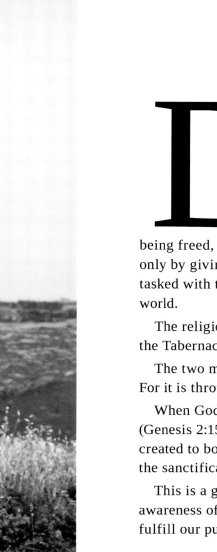

Depending on the context, the word *avodah* can mean either "work" or "service."

In Hebrew, worshiping God is called avodat Hashem and implies serving God through one's actions and choices. One who serves God is known as an eved Hashem, which means, literally, "a slave of God." The Israelites in Egypt were forced to be avadim (slaves) to the Egyptians but, upon being freed, became "slaves" to God. Slavery to God, however, is a blessing, for it is only by giving ourselves to God that we can truly be free. This "slavery" entails being tasked with the important mission of bringing knowledge of God and His word to the world.

The religious rituals performed thousands of years ago by the Priests and Levites in the Tabernacle and the Temple in Jerusalem were also referred to as *avodah*.

The two meanings of the word *avodah*, "working" and "serving," are closely related. For it is through our physical work that we serve God and bring Him honor.

When God placed Adam in the Garden of Eden, He placed Adam there l'ovdah (Genesis 2:15). This is the verb form of the word *avodah*, teaching Adam that he was created to both work and serve and that true service of God is accomplished through the sanctification of one's work.

This is a great lesson for all of us. By infusing our everyday work life with awareness of God, with thoughts about God, and with desire to connect to God, we will fulfill our purpose of serving God in every moment of our lives.

And Hashem God took the man and put him into the Garden of Eden, to **work** it and tend it.

(Genesis 2:15)

ויקח יהוה אלהים את האדם וינחהו בגן עדן

לעבדה ולשמרה.

"Six days you shall **labor** and do all your work."

(Exodus 20:9)

ששת ימים **תעבד** ועשית כל מלאכתך.

125

59

Song

Shirah (shee-RAH)

שִׁירָה

Shirah, Hebrew for "song," is a critical tool for drawing closer to God. The numerical equivalent of *shira*, song, is the same as that for *tefillah*, prayer, for a song that comes from the heart is a form of prayer to God.

When God saved the people of Israel and drowned the terrifying Egyptian army at the Reed Sea, the people sang to God. "Then Moses and the Israelites sang this song to God. They said: I will sing to God, for He triumphed gloriously; horse and driver He has hurled into the sea" (Exodus 15:1). After the awesome miracle of the splitting of the seat, mere words of thanks to God could not capture their emotions, and so Moses and the people burst into song.

The great Baal Shem Tov, the founder of the Hasidic movement in 18th-century Russia, used the power of song to inspire the downtrodden Jewish masses to feel the joy of God's love, despite their intense poverty and suffering at the hands of antisemites. He knew that the song of the soul would give the people strength to bear and overcome their suffering. Many students of the Baal Shem Tov went on to become Hasidic leaders in their own communities and composed their own songs of longing for God.

The Bible is also referred to as a song, as the verse says, "Therefore, write down this song and teach it to the people of Israel" (Deuteronomy 31:19). When read publicly in synagogues, the Bible is always chanted with ancient melodies that have been passed down for generations, melodies that help the congregation absorb the powerful words of the Bible.

"Then Moses and the Israelites **sang** this **song** to God. They said: I will **sing** to God, for He triumphed gloriously; horse and driver He has hurled into the sea."

(Exodus 15:1)

אז **ישיר** משה ובני ישראל את **השירה** הזאת ליהוה ויאמרו לאמר **אשירה** ליהוה כי גאה גאה סוס ורכבו רמה בים.

"Therefore, write down this **song** and teach it to the people of Israel; put it in their mouths, in order that this **song** may be My witness against the people of Israel."

(Deuteronomy 31:19)

ועתה כתבו לכם את **השירה** הזאת ולמדה את בני ישראל שימה בפיהם למען תהיה לי **השירה** הזאת לעד בבני ישראל.

60

Soul נְשָׁמָה

Neshamah (n'-sha-MAH)

hen describing the creation of Adam, the first man, the Bible says that God blew "into his nostrils the breath of life," a gift no other living being received. Jewish tradition teaches that each time we breathe, the original act of God breathing life into us is repeated.

Man's very breath came directly from God, infusing his being with a lofty soul capable of being conscious and aware of God's presence in the world. *Neshimah*, the Hebrew word for "breath," is composed of the same letters, in the same order, as *neshamah*, the Hebrew word for "soul." Our precious souls, the very essence of our being, are truly the breath of God.

"The soul of man is the candle of God, revealing all his innermost parts" (Proverbs 20:27). Rabbi Shneur Zalman of Liadi, an early Hasidic master, teaches that the human soul is literally a "piece" of God from above that is placed into each and every person. This Godly presence within us allows us to reveal our "innermost parts," helping us recognize the strengths that God blessed each of us with, as well as our incomplete parts that need further development and fixing.

The word *neshamah* appears in the very last verse of the very last psalm in the Book of Psalms. "Let all souls praise God, Hallelujah!" (Psalms 150:6). Praising God and recognizing that everything God does is for the good is the highest expression of the soul.

"The **soul** of man is the candle of God, revealing all his innermost parts."

(Proverbs 20:27)

נר יהוה **נשמת** אדם חפש כל חדרי בטן.

"God formed the human from the dust of the ground, blowing into his nostrils the **breath** of life: the Human became a living being."

(Genesis 2:7)

וייצר יהוה אלהים את־האדם עפר מן האדמה
ויפח באפיו **נשמת** חיים ויהי האדם לנפש חיה.

129

61

Spirit

Ruach (RU-akh)

רוּחַ

**R**uach, Hebrew for "spirit," appears in the second verse of the Bible as "a spirit of God sweeping over the water" at the very beginning of the creation of the world. Similarly, divine inspiration is known as *ruach hakodesh,* literally translated as "holy spirit."

The Sages teach that "a person does not sin unless a *ruach shtut,* a spirit of folly, enters him." Since a person's soul is from God and always connected to God, only a spirit foreign to his soul can cause him to sin.

In other contexts, *ruach* means "wind" or "breath." At the splitting of the sea, "God drove back the sea with a strong east wind (*ruach*) all that night, and turned the sea into dry ground" (Exodus 14:21). A few verses later, the word *ruach* appears again, this time meaning "breath." After the children of Israel cross safely to the other side, they sing, "At the breath of Your nostrils the waters piled up" (Exodus 15:8).

After Pharaoh increased the burden of the suffering Hebrew slaves in Egypt, Moses sought to comfort the people. "But when Moses told this to the Israelites, they would not listen to Moses, because of their shortness of breath (*ruach*) and the cruel bondage" (Exodus 6:9). Their enslavement caused them such physical and emotional stress that they were unable to breathe normally or maintain a sense of calm and focus. In this painful emotional state, they could not even absorb God's promise that they would soon be freed from their bondage.

"The earth being unformed and void, with darkness over the surface of the deep and a **spirit** from God sweeping over the water."

(Genesis 1:2)

והארץ היתה תהו ובהו וחשך על פני תהום ורוח
אלהים מרחפת על פני המים.

"But when Moses told this to the Israelites, they would not listen to Moses, because of their shortness of **breath** and because of the cruel bondage."

(Exodus 6:9)

וידבר משה כן אל בני ישראל ולא שמעו אל
משה מקצר רוח ומעבדה קשה.

62

Stranger

Ger *(gayr)*

The Hebrew word *ger* can mean "stranger," "foreigner" or "convert," all of whom are vulnerable outsiders often forced to live on the outskirts of society.

When Abraham asks the Hittites to sell him a burial plot for Sarah, he refers to himself as a *ger toshav*, a "resident stranger" in the land. The term appears to be a contradiction; if Abraham is a resident, then he is not a stranger, and if he is a stranger, then he is not a resident. But upon deeper contemplation, we see that Abraham's phrase captures the tenuousness of the human condition. Abraham calls himself a "stranger" in this world, for though he is alive right now, he recognizes that, like his wife Sarah, he will not live forever. At the same time, Abraham is a "resident" of this world, for he is still alive and capable of fulfilling his mission on earth.

Forced to flee from Egypt to the land of Midian, Moses referred to himself as a *ger* and chose a name for his son that reflected his outsider status. "He named him Gershom, for he said, "I have been a stranger in a foreign land" (Exodus 22:2).

In Biblical times, the word *ger* was often used to refer to people from other nations who were living within the borders of Israel. If these people renounced idol worship, they were permitted to stay and even protected by the laws of the Bible. "You too must befriend the stranger, for you were strangers in the land of Egypt" (Deuteronomy 10:19). God considers the Israelites' own experience as hated strangers in Egypt as the foundation for their responsibility and obligation to care for strangers within their own borders.

"I am a resident **stranger** among you; sell me a burial site among you, that I may remove my dead for burial."

(Genesis 23:4)

גר ותושב אנכי עמכם תנו לי אחזת קבר עמכם ואקברה מתי מלפני.

"You must befriend the **stranger**, for you too were **strangers** in the land of Egypt."

(Deuteronomy 10:19)

ואהבתם את הגר כי גרים הייתם בארץ מצרים.

63

Strength גְּבוּרָה

Gevurah (g'-vu-RAH)

Gevurah, the Hebrew word for "strength," is often used in the Book of Psalms to describe the greatness of God. An essential aspect of our praise and worship of God is understanding His strength and His ability to do anything He chooses to do.

Human beings can also possess gevurah. In Jewish thought, Isaac, the second of our patriarchs, is associated with this trait. But why is Isaac, who is nowhere described in the Bible as unusually strong, associated with the trait of *gevurah*?

In Jewish thought, *gevurah* refers primarily to spiritual strength and restraint, as opposed to physical strength - and it is Isaac's spiritual strength that set him apart. Isaac succeeded in subsuming his personal ego, fulfilling the mission that God gave him and which the world so desperately needed. He understood that it was his role to humbly continue in the path of his father Abraham. Isaac was not called upon to create his own, individual path, but rather to internalize his father's teachings, follow in his father's footsteps, and ensure the continuity of his father's legacy. He was proud to be "Isaac the son of Abraham" (Genesis 25:19).

The Talmud asks: "Who is the gibor, the person of strength? The one who conquers his negative desires." More than physical prowess, the Bible favors spiritual strength, the ability to overcome one's own self-centered desires for the sake of a much greater and more important goal.

"Who can tell the **mighty acts** of Hashem, proclaim all His praises?"

(Psalms 106:2)

מי ימלל **גבורות** יהוה ישמיע כל תהלתו?

"Thus said Hashem: let not the wise man glory in his wisdom; let not the **strong** man glory in his **strength**; let not the rich man glory in his riches."

(Jeremiah 9:22)

כה אמר יהוה אל יתהלל חכם בחכמתו ואל יתהלל **הגבור בגבורתו** אל יתהלל עשיר בעשרו.

64

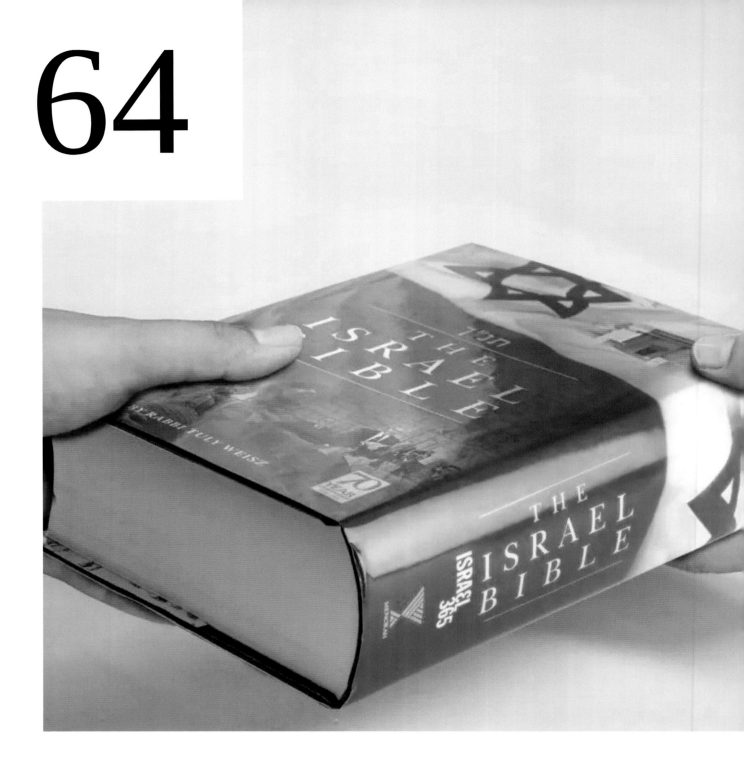

Study

Limmud (li-MUD)

לִמּוּד

L immud, Hebrew for "study," is a central pillar of Judaism. Knowledge of the Bible and what God expects of us is a vital prerequisite to living a holy life. For this reason, *talmud torah*, studying the Bible, is considered the most important of the Bible's 613 commandments. As the Talmud teaches, "study is great for it leads to action."

But studying the Bible is not only important for the sake of knowledge. Studying itself, like prayer, is a means to connect to God. It is not merely an academic endeavor, but rather a deeply spiritual one. As King David writes, "But the teaching of God is his delight, and he studies that teaching day and night" (Psalms 1:2).

Judaism stresses the value of education, and particularly the importance of parents teaching their children. "And teach them to your children, reciting them when you stay at home and when you are away, when you lie down and when you get up" (Deuteronomy 11:19). Jewish children are taught to read from a young age, a practice that only became more common throughout the world in recent centuries. Strong Bible education was the key to Jewish survival for two millennia of exile.

The late Rabbi Jonathan Sacks viewed study as crucial to proper and positive leadership. He said, "To be a Jewish leader means spending time to study both Torah and wisdom: wisdom to understand the world as it is, Torah to understand the world as it ought to be. Leaders should never stop learning. That is how they grow and teach others to grow with them."

"And **teach** them to your children, reciting them when you stay at home and when you are away, when you lie down and when you get up."

(Deuteronomy 11:19)

ולמדתם אתם את בניכם לדבר בם בשבתך בביתך ובלכתך בדרך ובשכבך ובקומך.

"And all your children shall be **students** of God, and great shall be the happiness of your children."

(Isaiah 54:13)

וכל בניך למודי יהוה ורב שלום בניך.

65

Tabernacle מִשְׁכָּן

Mishkan (mish-KAN)

Mishkan, Hebrew for "Tabernacle," refers to the holy sanctuary that God commanded the children of Israel to construct in the desert as a place of worship. The root of the word *Mishkan* means "to dwell," as the verse states, "And let them make Me a sanctuary that I may *dwell* among them" (Exodus 25:8). God's presence was felt and experienced in the *Mishkan* more than any other place on Earth. The Hebrew word for God's presence is *Shechinah,* which shares the same grammatical root as *Mishkan.*

The Sages teach that the *Mishkan* was an atonement for the sin of the golden calf. By worshiping the golden calf, the people demonstrated their faith in polytheism, the belief that there are many disparate forces in the world controlled by many gods. The *Mishkan* was an atonement for this sin, for it was a dwelling place for the one true God of the universe. In building this sanctuary, the people acknowledged that all of the forces of nature emanate from God alone.

The *Mishkan* was made of many different and disparate parts, including wood, various metals, fabrics and animal skins. Yet upon the completion of the *Mishkan,* the Bible declares that "the *Mishkan* was one whole" (Exodus 26:6), emphasizing that despite the great diversity of parts in the *Mishkan,* it possessed an inherent unity. The same is true of the entire world. Though the universe is unbelievably diverse, all of its creations were formed and created by God and are an expression of His will.

"On the day that the **Tabernacle** was set up, the cloud covered the **Tabernacle**, the Tent of the Pact; and in the evening it rested over the **Tabernacle** in the likeness of fire until morning."

(Numbers 9:15)

וביום הקים את **המשכן** כסה הענן את **המשכן** לאהל העדת ובערב יהיה על **המשכן** כמראה אש עד בקר.

"How fair are your tents, oh Jacob, your **dwellings,** oh Israel!"

(Numbers 24:5)

מה טבו אהליך יעקב **משכנתיך** ישראל.

66

Thanks

הוֹדָאָה

Hodaah (ho-da-AH)

Hodaah, the Hebrew word for "thanks," is also the root of the Hebrew word *Yehudi,* which means "Jew." In turn, *Yehudi* comes from the name of the tribe of *Yehudah,* "Judah", who was given this name by his mother Leah after she gave birth to more sons than she expected to have. She immediately expressed her deep gratitude for this gift, saying "This time I will praise God." In fact, the Rabbis teach that Leah was the first one to truly give *hodaah* to God.

She instilled this trait in Judah, who then passed on this trait to the Jewish people who, today, mostly descend from his tribe. As Rabbi Shlomo Carlebach taught, to be a Jew literally means to give thanks and express gratitude for all the blessings that fill our lives. In fact, one of the most important Jewish values is *hakarat hatov,* recognizing the good that others, including God, do for us. This is why King David writes over and over again through the Book of Psalms, "Give thanks to God, for He is good, His steadfast love is eternal" (Psalms 118:11).

Hodaah also means to be *modeh,* to "admit the truth," which Judah so humbly did in the story of his relationship with Tamar (Genesis 38:26). What is the connection between giving thanks and admitting the truth? The Sages teach that both giving thanks and admitting the truth require authentic humility before God. When we understand that everything comes from God, we will thank Him for all that we've been blessed with and will not allow our egos to stand in the way of admitting the truth.

She conceived again and bore a son, and declared, "This time I will **praise** God." Therefore she named him Judah. Then she stopped bearing."

(Genesis 29:35)

ותהר עוד ותלד בן ותאמר הפעם **אודה** את יהוה על כן קראה *שמו* יהודה ותעמד מלדת.

"Give **thanks** to God, for He is good, His steadfast love is eternal."

(Psalms 118:1)

הודו ליהוה כי טוב כי לעולם חסדו.

67

Trust

בִּטָּחוֹן

Bitachon (bi-ta-KHON)

Bitachon, "trust," is the backbone of our relationship with God. No matter what is happening in one's personal life or in the broader world, one who possesses *bitachon* trusts that everything comes from God. And because God is purely good, everything that happens is ultimately for the good. Acquiring *bitachon* requires internalizing the belief that there are no coincidences in the world. It is the denial of randomness and chance in our world. It means that whatever happens is a function of God's will and God's decree.

Bitachon, however, is different from faith. It's faith put into practice. "Trust in God and do good" (Psalm 37:3). The "doing good" that comes after one has trust in God is the overcoming of fear and worry that naturally results from experiencing a challenging experience or situation.

"Behold the God Who gives me triumph, I will trust, I will not be afraid" (Isaiah 12:2). When we trust in God we are not afraid, because we know that no matter what happens, God is there. We are not alone!

Bitachon means trusting in God's plan for humanity, even as secular culture grows more influential and many people turn away from God. "For My plans are not your plans, nor are My ways your ways, declares *Hashem*" (Isaiah 55:8). We must trust that salvation will one day come as promised.

There was a well known 1st century Jewish sage with an unusual name: *Nachum Ish Gamzu*, meaning "Nachum the 'also this' man." He was given this name because he was famous for always saying, "*Also this* is for the good." For one who has *bitachon* knows that no matter what happens, it is for the good.

"**Trust** in Hashem and do good, abide in the land and remain loyal."

(Psalms 37:3)

בטח ביהוה ועשה טוב שכן ארץ ורעה אמונה.

"Behold God is my salvation; I will **trust** and will not be afraid; for Hashem the Lord is my strength and might, and He is my deliverance."

(Isaiah 12:2)

הנה אל ישועתי אבטח ולא אפחד כי עזי וזמרת
יה יהוה ויהי לי לישועה.

68

Truth

אֱמֶת

Emet (e-MET)

Emet, Hebrew for "truth," is made up of three letters: *alef, mem,* and *tuf.* These letters are, in order, the first, middle and last letters of the Hebrew alphabet. The Sages teach that this shows us how truth is meant to encompass our entire lives, from the beginning, through the middle and until the very end.

God wants us to be open and truthful in our service to Him. As King David wrote in Psalms, "God is near…to all who call Him in truth" (145:18). God does not only desire our gratitude or our praise, but also wants us to share all that we are going through, from the depths of our hearts. God wants us to speak with Him as if we're speaking with a best friend. He wants us to share the truth of our entire beings and to know that it will be heard and received with nothing but love and compassion.

The prophet Zechariah calls Jerusalem "the city of truth," because in Jerusalem we feel and experience the presence of God in such a powerful and tangible way that we are inspired to live a life guided by the truth of God's word and God's will.

In Psalm 15, King David asks, "Who may sojourn in Your tent, who may dwell on Your holy mountain?" He answers, "He who lives without blame, who does what is right, and in his heart acknowledges the truth." Truth originates in the heart. From there it must spread outward to our speech and actions so that we align our complete selves with the truth of God's word.

"Thus said Hashem: I have returned to Zion, and I will dwell in Jerusalem, and Jerusalem will be called the city of **truth**, and the mount of Hashem of Hosts the Holy Mount."

(Zechariah 8:3)

כה אמר יהוה שבתי אל ציון ושכנתי בתוך

ירושלם ונקראה ירושלם עיר **האמת** והר יהוה

צבאות הר הקדש.

"God is near to all who call Him, to all who call Him in **truth**."

(Psalms 145:18)

קרוב יהוה לכל קראיו לכל אשר יקראהו **באמת**.

69

Vine

Gefen (GE-fen)

G efen, the Hebrew word for "vine," refers to grapes. Grapes are one of the seven well-known species of the land of Israel listed in Deuteronomy: "A land of wheat and barley, of vines, figs, and pomegranates, a land of olive trees and honey" (Deuteronomy 8:8).

In ancient Israel, grapes were primarily used for the production of wine, which was used for ritual purposes in sanctifying Shabbat and Jewish holidays throughout the year. The blessing said over wine ends with the words *borei pri ha'gefen,* "Who created the fruit of the vine."

Grapes play a central role in many stories throughout the Bible. While languishing in prison, Joseph interprets the dream of the royal cupbearer, who dreams about squeezing grapes into Pharaoh's cup. And when Moses sends twelve spies to surveil the land of Israel, they return with a cluster of grapes so large that many men are needed to carry it. This story is reflected in the modern State of Israel, where the official symbol of the Ministry of Tourism is an uncommonly large cluster of grapes being carried by two people.

Archaeologists in Israel have uncovered many ancient synagogues and other buildings that used grape vines as decorations on their stones. To this day, grape vines are seen as a symbol of prosperity and marital joy, as the verse states, "Your wife shall be like a fruitful vine within your house" (Psalms 128:3).

"A land of wheat and barley, of **vines**, figs, and pomegranates, a land of olive trees and honey."

(Deuteronomy 8:8)

ארץ חטה ושערה **וגפן** ותאנה ורמון ארץ־זית שמן ודבש.

"Your wife shall be like a fruitful **vine** within your house; your sons, like olive saplings around your table."

(Psalms 128:3)

אשתך **כגפן** פריה בירכתי ביתך בניך כשתלי זיתים סביב לשלחנך.

70

Water

Mayim (MA-*yim*)

מַיִם

*M*ayim, Hebrew word for "water," first appears in the second verse of the Bible when "the spirit of God hovered over the water." God does not explicitly command the creation of water, mysteriously present from the very beginning of time, reflecting its foundational role in the existence of all life.

Although water was used in many aspects of the Temple service, it was only brought as a stand alone offering to God during Sukkot, the Feast of Tabernacles. Each morning throughout the holiday, water was drawn from the Siloam spring, brought into the Temple and then poured on the main altar. Afterwards, every night in the Temple courtyard, thousands of people gathered for the *Simchat Beit HaShoeivah*, "Rejoicing at the Place of the Water-Drawing," a time of celebration, music and dancing.

The life of Moses, the greatest leader of Jewish history, is inextricably linked to water. When only a few months old, he was placed in a basket by his mother and set adrift on the Nile River in order to save him from Pharaoh's evil decree. Miraculously, Pharoah's very own daughter finds him, adopts him as her son and names him Moses, since she "drew him out of the water" (Exodus 2:10).

After fleeing Egypt, Moses meets his wife by a water well. Years later, Moses hits the rock in order to provide the nation with water, instead of speaking to it as God had commanded him to do. Tragically, this mistake cost Moses the opportunity to enter the Land of Israel, the land of life. Water is the source of life, but only if used in the service of God's will.

"For your God is bringing you into a good land, a land with streams of **water** and springs and fountains issuing from plain and hill."

(Deuteronomy 8:7)

כי יהוה אלהיך מביאך אל ארץ טובה ארץ נחלי

מים עינת ותהמת יצאים בבקעה ובהר.

"When the child grew up, she brought him to Pharaoh's daughter, who made him her son. She named him Moses, explaining, 'I drew him out of the **water**.'"

(Exodus 2:10)

ויגדל הילד ותבאהו לבת פרעה ויהי לה לבן

ותקרא שמו משה ותאמר כי מן **המים** משיתהו.

149

71

Weeks

שָׁבוּעוֹת

Shavuot (sha-vu-OT)

Shavuot, Hebrew for "weeks," is the name of one of the three pilgrimage festivals during which Jews in ancient Israel would travel to Jerusalem. Known as Pentecost in Greek, it is the only Jewish holiday whose date is not explicitly stated in the Bible. Instead, the Bible commands the people of Israel to count seven weeks from the second day of Passover, and the day after that, the 50th day, is the holiday of *Shavuot*. On *Shavuot*, God gave the Ten Commandments to the children of Israel.

The 49 days between Passover and *Shavuot* are counted in a daily ritual in anticipation of the great day when God gave the Bible to the people of Israel. *Shavuot* is traditionally celebrated by staying up all night long and studying the Bible until the sun rises the next morning.

Shavuot also means "oaths," for when God gave the Torah to the people of Israel He pledged His devotion to them, and they in turn committed to follow His commandments. Similarly, *Beer Sheva*, a southern Israeli city, means "Well of Oaths," for it was there that Abraham and King Abiimelech made vows of peace after quarreling over the rightful ownership of wells in that area.

The word *shavuot* is derived from the Hebrew word *sheva*, meaning "seven," the number of days in a week. Unlike the length of a year and the lunar month, which are based on the sun and the moon, there is nothing natural about the length of a week. The seven days of the week are rooted in the Biblical account of creation which has spread to all human cultures throughout the world.

"On the day of the first fruits, your Feast of **Weeks**, when you bring an offering of new grain to God, you shall observe a sacred occasion: you shall not work at your occupations."

(Numbers 28:26)

וביום הבכורים בהקריבכם מנחה חדשה ליהוה **בשבעתיכם** מקרא קדש יהיה לכם כל מלאכת עבדה לא תעשו.

"You shall count off seven **weeks**; start to count the seven **weeks** when the sickle is first put to the standing grain. Then you shall observe the Feast of **Weeks** for your God, offering your freewill contribution as your God has blessed you."

(Deuteronomy 16:9-10)

שבעה **שבעת** תספר לך מהחל חרמש בקמה תחל לספר שבעה **שבעות**. ועשית חג **שבעות** ליהוה אלהיך מסת נדבת ידך אשר תתן כאשר יברכך יהוה אלהיך.

72

Witness

עֵד

Eid (ayd)

The word *Eid*, "witness," is found in many different contexts, particularly in the Bible's extensive laws concerning testimony in a court of law. In fact, one of the Ten Commandments obligates us not to bear false witness, highlighting the seriousness of speaking only words of truth, particularly when they impact another person.

In almost all situations, Jewish courts require the testimony of two witnesses and will not accept the testimony of a single individual. This is to ensure that more than one perspective is taken into account as the court strives to reach the fairest verdict possible.

As human beings created in the image of God, we are charged with the task of bearing witness to God's creation of heaven and earth. While we can and should do this every day of our lives, *Shabbat*, the holy day of rest, is set aside as a day of bearing witness to God's act of creation. In the Jewish prayer book, *Shabbat* is called "a remembrance of the creation of the world."

In Judaism's most important prayer, the *Shema*, we also bear witness to the existence and oneness of God. The two Hebrew letters that make up the word *eid* appear in the words of the Shema itself. To highlight this connection, in the section of the Hebrew Bible where the *Shema* appears, these two letters are written larger than the other letters, ensuring we remember to bear witness to God as we recite the holy words of the *Shema*.

"You are My **witnesses**, declares *Hashem*, My servant, whom I have chosen. So that you may know and believe in Me, and understand that I am He: before Me no god was formed, and after Me none shall exist."

(Isaiah 43:10)

אתם **עדי** נאם יהוה ועבדי אשר בחרתי למען תדעו ותאמינו לי ותבינו כי אני הוא לפני לא נוצר אל ואחרי לא יהיה.

"You shall not bear false **witness** against your neighbor."

(Exodus 20:13)

לא תענה ברעך **עד** שקר.

73

Work

מְלָאכָה

Melachah (m'-la-KHAH)

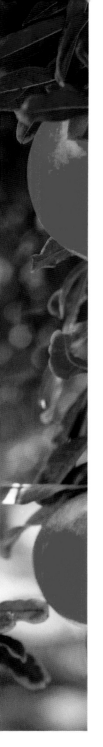

M*elachah*, Hebrew for "work," is central to a happy and meaningful life. The Talmud teaches, "All Torah study without work will result in waste and will cause sinfulness." Study and work are essential to living a balanced and grounded life dedicated to both spiritual pursuits and the building of the physical world.

When commanding *Shabbat* observance, the Bible repeatedly emphasizes that it is a day on which "you shall not do any work." Work is for the six days of the week, while *Shabbat* is set aside for rest. Refraining from creative work sanctifies the seventh day, for by resting we recognize that God is the creator of this world, as we acknowledge in prayer, "Through their rest they will sanctify Your name."

When commanding the Israelites to build the Tabernacle, God designated Bezalel to lead the holy project, for "I have endowed him with a divine spirit of skill, ability, and knowledge of all kinds of *melachah*" (Exodus 31:3). The construction of the Tabernacle involved 39 different categories of work, from dyeing to weaving to writing and burning. The work prohibited on *Shabbat* corresponds to the 39 categories of work performed by the Israelites in the construction of the Tabernacle. The Tabernacle represents the pinnacle of creative human accomplishment, and so we do not engage in these creative activities on *Shabbat*.

Melachah also refers to the Divine service performed in the Tabernacle by the Priests and Levites, as it says, "from the age of thirty years up to the age of fifty, all who are subject to service, to do work in the Tabernacle" (Numbers 4:3).

"But the seventh day is a Sabbath of your God: you shall not do any **work**—you, your son or daughter, your male or female servants, or your cattle, or the stranger who is within your settlements."

(Exodus 20:10)

ויום השביעי שבת ליהוה אלהיך לא תעשה כל **מלאכה** אתה ובנך ובתך עבדך ואמתך ובהמתך וגרך אשר בשעריך.

"Thus the Israelites, all the men and women whose hearts moved them to bring anything for the **work** that God, through Moses, had commanded to be done, brought it as a freewill offering to God."

(Exodus 35:29)

כל איש ואשה אשר נדב לבם אתם להביא לכל **המלאכה** אשר צוה יהוה לעשות ביד משה הביאו בני ישראל נדבה ליהוה.

155

74

World

Olam (o-LAM)

עוֹלָם

Olam, Hebrew for "world," is frequently used in the form of *l'olam*, meaning "forever." When the Bible describes God's dominion over the *olam*, the world, it does so by highlighting that God's dominion is *l'olam*, infinite and eternal.

Olam shares a grammatical root with the Hebrew word *ne'elam*, meaning "hidden." Jewish thinkers explain that many more worlds exist beyond the physical one that we experience in our everyday lives. These are the upper spiritual realms, including the realm of the angels, that both influence and are influenced by our physical world, specifically through human actions. The higher the world, the more singular it becomes, tending towards unity. At the very top of all of the worlds is the pure unity of God. To the human eye, however, the deeper aspects of our word remain hidden. We struggle to see and comprehend the way God is directly involved in each and every moment of our lives. The world's true reality remains hidden from our eyes.

The Kabbalists explain that God created the world in order to give, as the verse states, "I declare, 'A world of kindness will be built'" (Psalms 89:3). Before the world was created only God Himself existed, and there was no one to give to. God created the world so that there would be creations capable of receiving what He wants to give. "And God created man in His own image" (Genesis 1:27). By giving to others, man emulates his Creator and, together with God, fulfills the purpose of the world's creation.

"I declare, 'A world of kindness will be built; there in the heavens You establish Your faithfulness.'"

(Psalms 89:3)

כי אמרתי **עולם** חסד יבנה שמים תכן אמונתך בהם.

"A song of praise, of David: I will extol You, my God and king, and bless Your name forever and ever."

(Psalms 145:1)

תהלה לדוד ארוממך אלוהי המלך ואברכה שמך **לעולם** ועד.

157

Zion

Tzion (tzee-YON)

צִיּוֹן

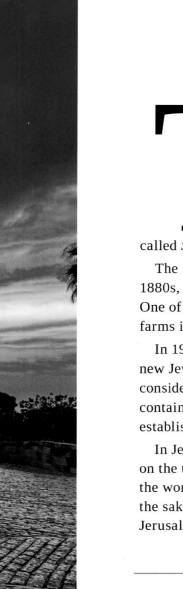

T*zion*, Hebrew for "Zion," most specifically refers to Mount Zion, one of the hills that surrounded ancient Jerusalem, but at times is also used interchangeably with Jerusalem. Zion also refers to the land of Israel generally, specifically regarding the longing of the Jews to return there from their exile in foreign lands. For this reason, the return of the Jewish people to Israel after the first Babylonian exile in the 6th century BCE was called *Shivat Tzion*, "Return to Zion."

The movement that inspired the modern return of Jews to Israel, beginning in the 1880s, is called Zionism, for it was inspired by the nation's ancient longing for Zion. One of the very first Zionist organizations that helped Jews buy land and establish farms in Israel during the late 19th century was called *Hibat Tzion*, or "Lovers of Zion."

In 1948, when Zionist leaders were preparing to declare the independence of the new Jewish state and debated what to call it, Zion was one of the leading names they considered. Though it was not ultimately chosen, many communities around Israel contain the name Zion, including one of the very first modern Jewish communities established in Israel, *Rishon L'Tzion*, meaning "First to Zion."

In Jewish liturgy it is written that "a redeemer shall come to Zion." This is based on the tradition that the Messiah will reign in Jerusalem and from there he will teach the world to know God and follow His righteous ways. The prophet Isaiah wrote, "For the sake of Zion I will not be silent" (Isaiah 62:1), for he understood the central role Jerusalem will play in the redemption of the world. May we soon see that day!

"By the rivers of Babylon, there we sat, sat and wept, as we thought of **Zion**."

(Psalms 137:1)

על נהרות בבל שם ישבנו גם בכינו בזכרנו את
ציון.

"For the sake of **Zion** I will not be silent, for the sake of Jerusalem I will not be still, till her victory emerges resplendent and her triumph like a flaming torch."

(Isaiah 62:1)

למען ציון לא אחשה ולמען ירושלים לא
אשקוט עד יצא כנגה צדקה וישועתה כלפיד
יבער.

About The Author

Rabbi Akiva Gersh teaches online classes and leads virtual Israel tours for Israel365. He is the editor of *Becoming Israeli,* a compilation of essays giving readers an inside look at the unique experience of making *Aliyah* and acclimating to life in Israel. In 2010, he created Holy Land Spirit, an uplifting spiritual and musical experience for Christian groups visiting Israel that fosters dialogue between Christians and Jews. Together with their four children, Akiva and his wife Tamar live in Pardes Hanna, Israel.

Connect to Israel on a deeper level with
The Israel Bible

The only Bible highlighting the special relationship between the Land and People of Israel. Through traditional and contemporary Jewish sources, *The Israel Bible* presents God's eternal and unchanging love for the Promised Land and His Chosen People from biblical times until today.

- 2,200 pages of side by side Hebrew and English
- Exclusive collection of maps, photos, charts and illustrations
- Hundreds of unique and inspiring study notes

Get your copy today at:
www.israel365store.com

For more inspiring
commentary, interactive maps,
educational videos, vivid
photographs and more, please
visit our website

www.TheIsraelBible.com